BARRIERS BETWEEN US

Cassandra Jackson

Barriers between Us

Interracial Sex in Nineteenth-Century American Literature

Indiana University Press
Bloomington and Indianapolis

This book is a publication of

Indiana University Press
601 North Morton Street
Bloomington, IN 47404-3797 USA

http://iupress.indiana.edu

Telephone orders 800-842-6796
Fax orders 812-855-7931
Orders by e-mail iuporder@indiana.edu

The paper used in this publication meets the minimum requirements of American National Standard for Information Sciences—Permanence of Paper for Printed Library Materials, ANSI Z39.48-1984.

Manufactured in the United States of America

Library of Congress Cataloging-in-Publication Data

Jackson, Cassandra, date
Barriers between us : interracial sex in nineteenth-century American literature / Cassandra Jackson.
p. cm. — (Blacks in the diaspora)
Includes bibliographical references and index.
ISBN 0-253-34511-1 (alk. paper) — ISBN 0-253-21733-4 (pbk. : alk. paper)
1. American fiction—19th century—History and criticism. 2. Racially mixed people in literature. 3. Miscegenation in literature. 4. Race in literature. I. Title. II. Series.
PS374.M84J33 2004
813'.3093552—dc22

2004007879

1 2 3 4 5 09 08 07 06 05 04

For Breona

Contents

Acknowledgments ix

Introduction: Race and Nation in Nineteenth-Century Interracial Fictions 1

1. *The Last of the Mohicans* or the First of the Mulattos? Slavery and Native American Removal in Cooper's American Frontier 9

2. A Land without Names: National Anxiety in *The Slave; or, Memoirs of Archy Moore* 30

3. Reconstructing America in Lydia Maria Child's *A Romance of the Republic* and Frances E. W. Harper's *Minnie's Sacrifice* 48

4. Doubles in Eden in George Washington Cable's *The Grandissimes* 71

5. "I will gladly share with them my richer heritage": Schoolteachers in Frances E. W. Harper's *Iola Leroy* and Charles Chesnutt's *Mandy Oxendine* 91

Epilogue: Formulating a National Self 113

Notes 119

Bibliography 133

Index 139

Acknowledgments

I am deeply indebted to many colleagues whose guidance contributed to the production of this book. I thank my advisor, Frances Smith Foster, whose advice and advocacy were critical to the birth of this book. I am also grateful to Mary Loeffelholz, whose precise and prompt responses to my work became the lens through which I learned that this project was indeed a book. I would like to thank Wayne Franklin for graciously allowing me to read his biography in progress on James Fenimore Cooper and for calling my attention to Cooper's *The Travelling Bachelor; or, Notions of the Americans.* Perhaps one chapter of this book might not have been written had it not been for William L. Andrews, who directed my attention to Charles Chesnutt's *Mandy Oxendine.* My thanks to those who read this manuscript in various stages, including Mark Sanders, Cris Levenduski, Sarah Robbins, Barbara Rodriguez, and the astute readers chosen by Indiana University Press. The encouragement and example of many of my colleagues at Northeastern University, including Guy Rotella, Marina Leslie, Beth Britt, and Laura Green, have been invaluable to this process. I would like to express my gratitude to Elizabeth Shea, whose luminous insights about her own book lit the way for mine. I am also very thankful for the advice and delightful company of the 2002–2003 fellows of the W. E. B. Du Bois Institute for Afro-American Research at Harvard University. Much thanks to Henry Louis Gates Jr. for granting me the opportunity to spend a year immersed in that intellectual playground. I am obliged to Northeastern University's Provost's Office and the New England Board of Higher Education for their support of this project.

BARRIERS BETWEEN US

Introduction: Race and Nation in Nineteenth-Century Interracial Fictions

In Frances E. W. Harper's novel *Iola Leroy* (1892), a white suitor proposes marriage to the nearly white title character, and she responds: "There are barriers between us that I cannot pass."[1] Harper's representation of barriers between these visibly white but theoretically racially different lovers suggests that race consisted not of phenotypic differences but rather prescribed classifications that define the legislative, civic, and social landscape of the United States. The heroine rejects a life as the white wife of a middle-class doctor, choosing instead to become a black activist devoted to achieving economic, civic, and social equality for former slaves. Her options highlight how the ideology of racial difference consisted of barriers that signify not only social distinctions but also civil ones, tracing the line between citizen and non-citizen, American and non-American, slave and free. Harper was not the first to employ black-white mixed-race characters to call attention to how American national identity was inflected by racial ideology. Throughout the nineteenth century, African-American and European-American writers explored political, social, and civil boundaries that defined the nation by depicting mixed-race figures. This study considers nineteenth-century stories of mulatto characters as narratives about the nation.

The representation of mulatto figures in nineteenth-century American literature reveals a rigorous discussion about the critical role of racial ideology in inventing an American identity. Valerie Babb's explanation of the ways in which the fiction of race was crucial to the formulation of American national identity illuminates my interpretation of fiction that includes mixed-race characters. According to Babb,

> From the 1700s on, whiteness is key to the maintenance of American nation-state identity. It replaced a cohesive Old World culture whose beliefs, traditions, and practices bound a people together over time. . . . Whiteness retained the "heat" of an unsettled, migrating people, grounding them, giving permanence and commonality of identity. To the different ethnicities and classes who left Europe to come to an unfamiliar wilderness where new structures had to be devised to meet new needs, whiteness furnished social order that forged a nascent national identity and minimized potential class warfare.[2]

The flip side of Babb's reading of whiteness is the way in which blackness functions, as Toni Morrison describes it, to "limn out" whiteness.[3] This interdependence between whiteness and blackness as they relate respectively to concepts of American and not-American demonstrates the way in which race articulates nation in the United States. The presence of mulatto figures, whose perceived whiteness and imputed blackness allowed them to skate on this boundary so critical to the construction of national identity, functions as a lens through which to magnify and investigate this relationship between race and nationhood.

Despite the rich intersections between mixed-race figures and constructions of national identity, African-American poet and critic Sterling Brown's 1937 dismissal of mulatto figures as what he termed the "tragic mulatto" dominated the critical discussion of mixed-race characters for years. According to Brown, what made these characters tragic was that though they were nearly white, these intelligent, courageous men and extraordinarily beautiful women were condemned to bondage, making their enslavement seem more unfortunate than that of pure blacks. To Brown, this melodramatic stereotype of a nearly white, withering woman or a rebellious man doomed to tragedy by his conflicted blood was devoid of social critique and represented nothing more than the racism of white writers and audiences who could only sympathize with white heroes and heroines.[4] While over time critics have revisited the figure, Brown's tag and his reading of the character as a concession to white audiences has lingered. Indeed, more critical attention has been paid to who used "the tragic mulatto," black or white writers, than to a more fundamental question of whether or not this configuration is in fact the dominant mode of mixed-race fiction.[5] The persistence of Brown's interpretation is evident in more recent critical readings of mixed-race figures. Carolyn Karcher suggests that Lydia Maria Child's use of the "tragic mulatto" was an attempt to garner the support of her white abolitionist audience. Black writers have come under particular scrutiny for their supposed attention to white audiences reflected in their use of mixed-race characters. Deborah McDowell attributes Harper's use of nearly white characters to pandering to a white audience.[6] Similarly, Houston Baker accuses black writers who use these figures of "an implicit approval of white patriarchy inscribed in the very features of the mulatto character's face."[7]

While I do not want to suggest that no nearly white character was intended to appeal to white audiences, I propose that to focus on this interpretation assumes a monolithic audience and dismisses the diverse characterization and narratological fluidity of mulatto fiction. As Ann Ducille points out, the assumption that mixed-race characters were primarily produced with the intention of garnering white audiences discounts the mulatto fiction published in black periodicals, such as the *Christian Recorder*.[8] In addition, the incendiary potential of these pale faces that confronted sexual violence, interracial desire, and racial fluidity should not be underestimated. Indeed, the estimation of publishers of the *Atlantic* that Charles Chesnutt's *Mandy Oxendine* was not "a safe venture," a decision that initiated the 100-year gap between the composition of the manuscript in the 1890s and the publication of the novel in 1994, suggests that rather than appeasing white audiences, these characters were capable of challenging prevailing ideologies of race. Finally, the diversity among characters and narratives that appear in mulatto fiction compels a more textually specific analysis, and one that addresses the complexities of particular cultural moments engaged by the literature.

Indeed, the "the" still used frequently before the term "mulatto" reflects the core of Brown's critique, that a single definable character reemerges in text after text. The methodological assumption of sameness implied by "the mulatto" is contradicted by the diversity of characterization that emerges among mixed-race figures. Werner Sollors notes that in the literature of the so-called tragic mulatto, "the text in front of us only rarely seems to fit the stereotype that it supposedly so rigidly and unchangingly and ineluctably embodies."[9] Jean Fagan Yellin, Ann Ducille, and Suzanne Bost also point to numerous exceptions to the narrative associated with the ill-fated tragic mulatto, particularly in works by African-American writers.[10] Works of fiction by European-American writers that includes mixed-race characters present these discrepancies as well. Even Child, whom Yellin credits with the invention of the tragic mulatto, presents two mixed-race heroines who prosper in her novel *A Romance of the Republic.*[11]

While mulatto figures form a recognizable stereotype by the similarities of the bodies they inhabit, the fluidity that distinguishes them suggests more than a fixed figure designed to pander to white audiences. Instead, it suggests a complex vehicle for discussions of racial difference. It is through this matrix of similarity of bodies and difference in characterization and narrative that writers of mulatto fiction make meaning. Mulatto figures function in much the same way that Jane Tompkins describes the literary stereotype: "Stereotypes are the instantly recognizable representatives of overlapping racial, sexual, national, ethnic, economic, social, political, and religious categories; they convey enormous amounts of cultural information in an extremely condensed form."[12] Straddling the boundaries that determined the building block of American citizenship, mulatto figures offered writers an abbreviation that signified the relationship between race and nationhood. The differences in how writers deployed these figures, however, demonstrate the diversity of their meditations on this issue. Hazel Carby, among others, has pointed out the potential of mulatto figures for social critique, arguing that as an expression of the relationship between the races, they posed challenges to the increasingly institutionalized segregation of the Jim Crow era.[13] While I agree with Carby that the increasing frequency of these figures during this era is a reflection of institutionalized racism, I want to propose that by the time that post-Reconstruction writers were producing mulatto fiction, mixed-race characters already functioned as complex cultural signs of the contradictions posed by a nation that had constructed its essential identity as free in the midst of slavery and racial exclusion. Mulatto figures not only allowed writers to discuss the relationship between the races, they were also ruminations on the national consequences of that relationship. Mulatto figures had long provoked consideration of the ways in which racial ideology shaped national policy and social and political relationships.

Because of the position of mulatto figures as the descendants of both blacks and whites, the figures suggested that the problems of slavery and Jim Crow were not "Negro" problems but rather a national problem that shaped the national character. At stake in solving problems such as slavery, segregation, and disenfranchisement was more than the future of African Americans; at issue was the fulfillment of a national creed of liberty and equality. The "Negro" problem might have been more accurately termed the American problem, because it represented the failure of the American experiment. To resurrect the dream of America, the nation had to first solve the race problem, somehow reconciling the national mantra with the national practice. Mulatto figures served as "cultural shorthand" for this national dilemma.[14] While some writers' depiction of mixed-race characters sought to imagine resolution between the larger narrative of American freedom and the enslavement of Africans in the United States, for others, mulatto figures operated as signs of America's most egregious sins, posing a counterargument to mythical representations of America as a new Eden. Mulatto characters could spoil the reverie of a cultural myth, reminding readers of the inequity between social reality and a very seductive modern mythology. While they called attention to slavery and sexual violence, often capturing the physical and psychological torment that owning bodies entailed, they also represented the literal and figurative blackening of a nation, a sure sign to many of the utter failure of the experiment in the wilderness.[15] Writers often illustrated this contradiction through the portrayal of mulatto characters in settings reminiscent of Eden. Lydia Maria Child, W. W. Smith, William Wells Brown, George Washington Cable, Mark Twain, and many others depicted variations on this theme, often posing the image of an American Eden contaminated by the evils of slavery. By employing racially ambiguous characters within this context, writers could contest the legitimacy of the critical role of racial distinctions in America. Mulatto figures embodied this contradiction, disturbing America's profound denial of racial mixing and disputing the myth of racial purity that had become central to the American civil system.

Some depictions of mulatto figures in Eden offered a critique of the idea of an American Adam by demonstrating the importance of origins in a land defined by race. Mulatto figures stood as a provocative challenge to the notion of the American Adam figure, who was "happily bereft of ancestry, untouched and undefiled by the usual inheritances of family and race."[16] As Sollors has noted,

> [T]his new [mulatto] character was a living challenge to the central contradiction of the New World, where the antiaristocratic promise of abandoning hereditary systems in favor of self-made men clashed with slavery and segregation, which reinstated a particularly sharp focus on the question of a character's ancestry.[17]

Mulatto figures in Eden demonstrated the fallacy of Adamic racelessness, or the notion of the American citizen abstracted from bodily identity. To be "undefiled by . . . family and race" in a country in which the marker of race formed the basis of the slave system, one would have to be both physically and ideologically white. The phenotypic whiteness and imputed and statutory blackness of mulatto figures demonstrated that this racelessness was a camouflage for a constructed notion of whiteness. In her critical study *Playing in the Dark,* Morrison suggests that perhaps at the root of the American Adam and the characteristics he expresses—innocence, alienation, domination—is what she calls an "Africanist presence," or a constructed notion of blackness against which the American Adam is defined.[18] Perhaps then, one might read the insertion of the mulatto figure into Eden as a desire to confront that Africanist presence, to unveil the hidden blackness that operates as the flip side, the not me, through which self-definition is constructed. The mulatto figure in Eden pinpoints the questions Morrison asks: "What . . . are Americans alienated from? What are Americans always so insistently innocent of? Different from?"[19]

Mulatto figures, while they call attention to the constructedness of blackness and whiteness, also emphasize the ways in which the fallacy of the readability of bodies was critical to constructions of American nationhood. According to Karen Sánchez-Eppler, by the 1830s, a focus on bodily identity in American literature exposed the bodily discrimination embedded in the civil structure, posing a challenge to assumptions of abstract political identity. No figures better captured the centrality of bodily identity within the national civil structure than mulatto characters, whose bodies were alienated from their prescribed identities. Indeed, the hyperembodiment of mulatto figures, which was exemplified by myths of racial signs, such as half-moon fingernails and "mezzotinto" eyes, that could supposedly disambiguate race demonstrate how mulatto figures present bodies whose slipperiness and ambiguity required that they be read or rendered intelligible according to conventional categories and at the same time resisted that kind of reading.[20] As Sánchez-Eppler puts it,

> The fictional mulatto combines this problematics of corporeality and identity for both [feminist and abolitionist projects] because miscegenation and the children it produces stand as a bodily challenge to the conventions of reading the body, thus simultaneously insisting that the body is a sign of identity and undermining the assurance with which that sign can be read.[21]

This resistance to the categories that underpin the civil structure designates each mulatto figure as what Lauren Berlant calls "a national subject, the paradigm problem citizen."[22] Paradoxically suspended between citizen and alien inhabitant, mulatto figures more than pointed to racial categories, they embodied the civil structure that depended on those categories while also challenging the legitimacy of that system.

This is not to suggest that all mulatto figures were intended to counter the prevailing racial ideology of the nineteenth century but rather to suggest that mixed-race characters were a way for writers to enter the conversation about the role of racial ideology in the United States. The resonance of mixed-race characters with matters of national identity allowed writers to use them to speak to particular cultural moments. This study traces mulatto figures throughout the nineteenth century, not because it presumes these figures were a static literary convention but rather because it argues that they were products of and vehicles for particular political and social ideas. For example, when Lydia Maria Child published her short story "The Quadroons" (1842), its narration of death and devastation of mixed-race characters can be read as a forewarning to antebellum America, while her Reconstruction-era novel *A Romance of the Republic* (1867) presents mixed-race characters who thrive in the aftermath of slavery, reflecting hope for national reconciliation. In addition, mulatto figures reveal the wide spectrum of concerns informed by regional, class, racial, and generational differences within the same period. For example, in his Reconstruction-era short story "Octoroon Slave of Cuba" (1871), Thomas Detter, a black writer from the western United States, demonstrates a concern with how the individual combats the economics of racism, while in *Minnie's Sacrifice* (1869), Frances E. W. Harper calls attention to the necessity of personal sacrifices, including financial ones, in the communal effort to build free black communities after the war.

This study seeks to explore the diversity of mixed-race figures, reading them not as part of a single narrative but rather as a shared rhetorical tool that initiated intertextual, interracial dialogue. By considering not only cross-racial variations but also intraracial, generational, gender, and regional differences and similarities in these works, this study seeks to explore the possibility of a conversation between a diverse group of writers, contextualizing the work of well-known writers by offering what might be described as the other half of the conversation. As Ducille points out, intertextuality must be viewed as "cutting across racial identities, cultural spaces, and historical moments" rather than conversations within isolated groups.[23] Mulatto figures, who embody just such a piercing of categories, offer rich intersections of race, region, and time. They present a fertile site in which to consider American writers in a wider context that perhaps revises the understanding of these works.

Chapters 1 and 2 consider pre–Civil War fiction. Chapter 1 examines James Fenimore Cooper's *The Last of the Mohicans* (1826), arguing that through Cora, Cooper injects slavery into the center of the national conversation about the expulsion of Native Americans. His novel anticipates the explosion of early abolitionist and antiremovalist discourse, which linked the two issues to exemplify the American failure to uphold its principles of freedom. Cooper develops a narrative of Cora's origins that casts slavery as an inheritance from Europe in an attempt to distance it from the American frontier and in doing so to situate European-American wars against Native Americans, not slavery, as the definitive American experience. Chapter 2 focuses on Richard Hildreth's *The Slave; or, Memoirs of Archy Moore* (1836). Though it is cited by many as the first antislavery novel, this fictionalized first-person narrative of a nearly white slave also reveals a wide range of social anxieties about the state of the nation. The chapter explores how for Hildreth, racial fluidity caused by slavery becomes a metaphor to explore the growing class fluidity of the 1830s.

The last three chapters consider post–Civil War fiction. Chapter 3 explores Reconstruction texts through a cross-section of mulatto fiction, including Lydia Maria Child's *A Romance of the Republic* and Frances E. W. Harper's recently rediscovered novel *Minnie's Sacrifice* (1869). For years little was believed to have been produced by African-American writers during the Reconstruction era, and Harper's novel fills crucial gaps in our understanding of American literature. The chapter explores these works as narratives of national regeneration. They offer solutions to the problem of racial inequity in the new nation. Chapters 4 and 5 consider post-Reconstruction mulatto fiction. Chapter 4 examines how southern writer George Washington Cable explores the interdependence of blackness and whiteness in constructions of national identity by pairing mulatto figures with white siblings. Chapter 5 addresses the way in which Charles Chesnutt and Frances E. W. Harper depict mixed-race characters to explore the African-American community's theory and practice in resisting the effects of racism. Harper's *Iola Leroy* (1892) and Chesnutt's *Mandy Oxendine* (believed to have been written in the 1890s) both portray mulatto figures as teachers to consider the role of black leadership in the struggle for social, civic, and economic equality. By merging the figure of a black schoolteacher, a symbol of black leadership, with a mulatto character, who has the option to pass as white and abandon black communities, these writers highlight the tension between communal duty and personal ambition.

This study is not an attempt to catalogue the wealth of mixed-race characters; rather, it examines closely several interracial fictions in light of the larger representation of race and nationhood in the United States. In a nation where citizenship is determined by racial identity, mixed-race characters circled the very core of the social structure and thus had the potential to challenge the legitimacy of the nation. This examination considers mulatto figures as literary devices that unfold social, cultural, and political ideas. Examining these figures as familiar cultural signs that raise a particular set of ideas within a culture, this study considers how writers posit mulatto figures to participate in a dialogue about the American condition.

1

The Last of the Mohicans or the First of the Mulattos? Slavery and Native American Removal in Cooper's American Frontier

In April of 1831, the confluence of removal and slavery was captured in the new masthead of the antislavery newspaper *The Liberator.* Only four months after the paper's first publication, William Lloyd Garrison added a picture that depicted a slave sale on its masthead. Distraught slaves collect at the picture's center, while interested consumers surround them. Trampled beneath the feet of a buyer lies a paper inscribed "Indian treaties." Behind this paper, a slave tied to a stake is being beaten. The U.S. Capitol building stands in the background with a flag reading "Liberty" flying overhead.[1] Though this depiction of Indian treaties among the scenes of slavery may seem like a curious addition to an antislavery newspaper's masthead, this pairing demonstrates the growing alliance between the early antislavery movement and antiremoval campaigns. By depicting Indian treaties as having been trodden underfoot by a slaveowner, the masthead illustrated the mutually beneficial relationship between the practice of slavery and Indian removal. Removal created a higher demand for slaves to clear newly acquired lands, and slavery provided the labor to ensure that the land acquisition would be profitable.[2] By combining the slave sale and the allusion to the appropriated lands of Native Americans, the masthead suggests that the cross-fertilization of racial ideology and commercial interests was driving both removal and slavery. The masthead denies the notion of particularized racial inferiorities as a justification for either practice, pointing rather to a national problem of racial discrimination.

The contrast between the masthead's background and foreground points to a national contradiction, illustrating the ways in which racial ideology determined U.S. national identity. In the issue which debuted the new masthead, an article calls the reader's attention to the image and interprets it lest the reader fail to understand its objective. The author points out the details of its composition, including its depiction of the Indian treaties among the scenes of slavery, and concludes, "Is it not delightful to know, that the Fourth of July is at hand, when we may laud ourselves and our country above all nations, and indignantly point the finger of scorn at foreign oppression? O Consistency! Thou art a precious jewel!"[3] This sardonic rhetorical question conveys what is illustrated in the masthead, that together removal and slavery posed unanswerable challenges to the nationally embraced mantra of freedom.

Five years before Garrison published *The Liberator,* James Fenimore Cooper addressed the national implications of slavery and removal in his novel *The Last of the Mohicans* (1826). Cooper introduces a character widely considered to be the first mulatto figure in an American novel in a text that takes as its subject the dispossession of Native Americans.[4] Through the insertion of Cora, the mixed-race descendant of slaves, into the novel, Cooper presents a narrative representation of the American experiment, or a map of how whites and nonwhites can (or perhaps cannot) function in one nation practically and ideologically. Cooper's treatment of slavery and removal anticipated the explosion of early abolitionist and antiremovalist discourse, which linked the two issues to exemplify the American failure to uphold its principles of civil rights and democracy. The narrative of slavery and removal that emerges in Cooper's novel, however, is concerned with reconciling the nationally embraced ideal of freedom with the practices of removal and slavery by excluding blacks and Indians from Americanness. As Valerie Babb argues, the equation of whiteness with supposedly authentic Americanness implied that "whites have a proprietary right to national resources and the allocation of these resources."[5] This projection of alienness onto African Americans and Native Americans provided justification for the appropriation of their labor and land. Cooper's text disputes the national implications of slavery and removal; it seeks to differentiate the two practices by carefully distinguishing Native Americans and African Americans as both racially distinct and extraneous to American nationhood.

While much of the criticism of Cooper's work has focused on its articulation of an American ethos of exploration, acquisition, and self-reliance, few critical treatments have considered Cora's ancestry in relation to these issues. Instead, criticism on Cora has either disregarded Cora's African ancestry or focused on her potential sexual relationships as explorations of miscegenation. Jane Tompkins describes Cora as a representation of white civilization, while David Haberly reads her as becoming "indianized."[6]

Leslie Fiedler has focused on the erotic energy that Cora's racialized sexuality contributes to the novel, arguing that the novel's "secret theme" is miscegenation, which Cooper fears.[7] George Dekker agrees that miscegenation is the theme of the novel; however, he contends that it is no secret, as Fiedler suggests. Rather, the romance between the Native American Uncas and Cora is a trial of the possible union of three races in the future United States. Dekker argues that the novel suggests that the future lies with Major Heyward and Alice, who will not only give birth to white children "but will also own plenty of Negro slaves."[8]

While Fiedler and Dekker offer valid points about the role of miscegenation in the novel, I would suggest that Cooper's representation of Cora and Uncas is concerned not only with the practical future of the three races but also with the theoretical implications that slavery and Native American removal together suggested for the ideological construction of a national identity. Cooper's novel justifies the discontinuities between slavery, removal, and democracy by externalizing the origins of slavery and essentializing black and red identities. By representing Cora as the descendant of West Indian slaves and the Scottish Colonel Munro, Cooper attempts to dissolve this connection, tracing the roots of American slavery back to European imperialism. Cooper distances slavery from the American frontier by locating it as a European institution, simultaneously differentiating America from Europe and positioning U.S. wars against Native Americans, not slavery, as the definitive American experience. As Fiedler points out, *The Last of the Mohicans* and many other novels published between 1826 and 1829 were primarily concerned with the relationship between America and Europe and with relations between white Americans and Native Americans.[9] Cora is not a "secret theme"; she is central to this conversation about national identity, which triangulates slavery, Native American removal, and Europe.

In addition, while *The Last of the Mohicans* depicts Native Americans, on the one hand, and Europe, on the other, as entities that serve to define what is and is not American, African-American slaves become the additional foreign entity against which the American identity must be defined. By distinguishing between black and red, Cooper's novel particularizes slavery and removal as outgrowths of essential racial properties, denying a generalized problem of racial inequity. Through the insertion of Cora, Cooper perhaps acknowledges the tendency to correlate the treatment of both groups, but by carefully delineating difference, he also justifies the exclusion of each group from whiteness and thus their exclusion from the privileges of American citizenship.

Slavery and Native American Removal

Cooper's concern with removal and slavery mirrors the tide of American political concern. In 1826, the same year that Cooper's novel was published, James Madison wrote: "Next to the case of the black race within our bosom, that of the red on our borders is the problem most baffling to the policy of our country."[10] Madison's coupling of these two issues, while it configures African Americans as integral to white domestic life and Native Americans as an external threat to that life, also suggests an integral relationship between "bosom" and "borders," or rather between the growth of the slavocracy and the expansion of national boundaries. Madison's pairing of slavery and Native American removal demonstrates their connectedness both as issues crucial to determining national policy and as interdependent practices. That white southerners supported expansionism precisely because of its implications for the extension of slave territory illustrates this interdependence.[11]

Both slavery and removal were becoming increasingly prominent concerns by the 1820s. The growing importance of slavery to the southern economy had already heightened debate over the institution.[12] During the first three decades of the nineteenth century, American slavery saw extraordinary growth. Cotton production was ten times greater than it had been at the beginning of the century, and the slave population had doubled during the first thirty years of the century. According to Herbert Aptheker, these developments contributed to the first major national governmental crisis involving slavery.[13] By the 1820s, the issue of slavery had culminated in congressional debates over the entry of the Missouri territory as a slave state in the Union. One of the central points of debate was the contradiction between American principles of democracy and the institution of slavery, a hypocrisy that became increasingly embarrassing to Americans as antislavery campaigns gained international exposure in the 1820s.[14]

At the same time, Native American removal was receiving more attention than antislavery in the American press. Indeed, the first American antislavery novel, Richard Hildreth's *The Slave; or, Memoirs of Archy Moore,* would not be published until 1836, during the rise of the American abolitionist movement. In contrast, the work of Cooper, Lydia Maria Child, Catherine Maria Sedgwick, and others published in the 1820s and 1830s suggest the already wide interest in removal policy. The possibility of a government policy of removal had been introduced in 1803, when Thomas Jefferson proposed a constitutional amendment validating the Louisiana Purchase while also making provisions for the removal of the tribes living east of the Mississippi to upper Louisiana. Between 1789 and 1829, the

U.S. government had bribed, deceived, and threatened to encourage Native American removal without the designation of an official removal policy.[15] During the 1820s, rapid expansion of white settlements was making isolation of Native Americans east of the Mississippi impossible, and the James Monroe administration revisited the possibility of a removal policy as a permanent solution to the problem. In 1825, the Senate passed a removal bill, but the bill did not pass in the House. Under the Andrew Jackson administration these issues came to a head, and another removal bill became law in 1830.[16]

The connection between the issues surrounding slavery and Native American removal was obvious to many. As early as 1825, Lydia Maria Child had pointed to the similarities between the issues. In *The Christian Indian; or, The Times of the First Settlers,* Child pointed to both issues as examples that the entire nation had fallen short of its principles:

> To those who would assert the lenity of the northern settlers, and would compare the slow inroads of these to the sappings of a nation's fall with the bloody acts and wanton cruelties of their precedents of southern America, it is indeed admitted they may boast for the former a record less black with iniquity, but their means, though comparatively those of men, have still terminated the same end.[17]

Child's comparison highlights how these issues operated together as an admission of national failure rather than just a southern one. While her references to the "means of . . . men" in her description of Indian conflict point to the popular conception of Indian wars as competition rather than land appropriation, she challenges this distinction as she draws the comparison to slavery.

Child was not alone in drawing such a comparison between slavery and removal. Indeed, they became increasingly more frequent as the antiremoval campaigns mobilized. John Greenleaf Whittier wrote in an essay on the necessity of abolition that "[t]he curse of slavery is enough to seal our eternal infamy; the unjust ejectment of Indians will be a crime which men may never forget, nor eternal justice forgive." Alexis de Tocqueville pointed to the similarities between the treatment of the two groups: "Both of them occupy an equally inferior position in the country they inhabit; both suffer from tyranny; and if their wrongs are not the same, they originate from the same authors."[18] The coverage of Indian affairs in abolitionist newspapers such as the *Pennsylvania Freeman* and the *Philadelphia National Enquirer* suggests recognition of the intersections between the two.[19] William Lloyd Garrison, editor of the antislavery paper *The Liberator* and co-editor of *Ge-*

nius, gave regular attention to Indian removal.[20] Many activists who would later become active in abolitionist campaigns were first involved in antiremoval efforts. James G. Birney, who had served as lawyer for the Cherokee in the 1820s, shortly after became involved in antislavery campaigns. In his biography of Birney, Beriah Green, a contemporary, explained Birney's involvement in both campaigns thus: "He could hardly fail to see . . . when the wrong of the Indians had thoroughly aroused him that the sufferings of the Negro flowed from the same bitter fountain."[21] James Russell Lowell, Angelina Weld Grimke, Harriet Beecher Stowe, Theodore Weld, Beriah Green, Arthur Tappan, and William Lloyd Garrison were all involved in both campaigns.[22] Linda Kerber has pointed out that this confluence of participants in both movements suggests that their activism was based not only on their understanding of slavery or removal but also on their recognition of the country's larger failure in race relations.[23]

The correlation between the treatment of Native Americans and African Americans is also apparent in the demise of the colonization movement.[24] Much like the removal of Native Americans, this campaign contended that the solution to the race problem would be the removal of racial difference from the United States by exporting blacks. Even though the movement focused on developing black colonies in West Africa, in 1825 Rep. George Tucker of Virginia suggested that Indian lands be purchased on behalf of free blacks who would establish colonies.[25] Ultimately, support for the colonization movement was dampened by antiremoval campaigns. Many of those who had initially supported colonization but eventually withdrew their support were also antiremovalists, including Lydia Maria Child, Arthur Tappan, Benjamin Lundy, Angelina Grimke, Theodore Weld, and William Lloyd Garrison.[26] Garrison made the comparison clear in his *Thoughts on African Colonization* (1832): "[African Americans] are as unanimously opposed to a removal to Africa, as the Cherokees from the council-fires and graves of their fathers."[27]

It should not be surprising that in the early nineteenth century, activists recognized these connections, particularly since the Seminole Wars in 1817–1818 and 1835–1842 made the interdependence of the two issues apparent. Both wars were deeply entangled with the slavery issue, because the blacks who lived among the Seminoles, often referred to as Seminole Negroes, were viewed by many as a threat to the institution of slavery. Kenneth Wiggins Porter argues that though the first of the Seminole Wars may have been initiated by general American expansionism, the desire to safeguard slavery was an increasingly important objective in the federal government's perpetration of these wars.[28] The presence of blacks in Indian settlements both encouraged and restrained American expansion. Slaveholders were disinclined to move their slaves into new territories that were near maroon colonies, and they urged the federal government to take action against such communities.[29] Slaves who escaped from their owners by fleeing to Seminole lands fueled the tension between the Seminoles and the federal government. Carter G. Woodson points out that "the agitation for the return of the Negro slaves . . . was kept up throughout [the 1820s] as a reason for removal."[30] Porter contends that the second Seminole War was "certainly a Negro war," intended to remove maroon settlements of blacks even more so than the Seminoles.[31] Legislators such as John Quincy Adams and Joshua Giddings attempted to circumvent the gag rule against speaking of slavery in Congress by using the Seminole Wars as a way of addressing the issue; such actions point to the relationship between the two subjects.[32] The Seminole Wars called attention to the issue of whether or not the government had an obligation to protect slavery and what authority the government should have over the institution in its propagation or abolition.

The African-American newspaper *The Colored American* reported on the second Seminole War, demonstrating African-American interests in the Florida conflict. Despite the paper's struggling budget, which forced them to omit the publication of numerous issues, the editors continued to use space to provide updates on the Seminole Wars. The paper published several installments of Joshua Giddings's 1841 speech to the House of Representatives; Giddings argued that the principle cause of the war was the federal government's desire to protect slavery.[33] In an 1838 article signed B. and probably contributed by Phillip A. Bell, the paper's founder, the author included the Seminole Wars as he noted the year's events that were relevant to the cause of antislavery: "The Seminole is still hunted and slain for his sickly, marshy swamps, driven from the home of his childhood, from the soil consecrated by the graves of his fathers, to pamper the already glutted appetite of the American for lands which he can never inhabit."[34] The paper also advertised and sold a lithograph entitled "The Bloodhounds," which depicted dogs being used to attack Seminoles. The ad demonstrates the connection between antislavery and antiremoval: "N. Southard . . . who always turns everything to anti slavery account . . . has got up a lithographic print, giving striking exhibition of the first fruits of the bloodhounds in Florida . . . in a manner calculated to excite the indignation of every mind. . . . Our readers ought to have it."[35]

Another item in 1841 illustrates the political connections between the interests of African Americans and Native Americans. A piece encouraging blacks to emigrate to Wisconsin reads: "We learnt that the Indians residing in Brothertown in this Territory have been admitted to the rights of citizenship. . . . The same rights will no doubt be extended to any other class of our proscribed countrymen. Brethren this is no doubt a free spot. . . . Now is the time to emigrate."[36] The author situates Native Americans in relationship to the pursuit of citizenship, as opposed to sovereignty. Cheryl Walker argues that much Native American literature demonstrated a concern for Native American citizenship and the discourse of nation, refuting the traditional assumption that the discourse of sovereignty dominated Native American cultural thought.[37] The attempts of both groups to debunk the association between whiteness and American citizenship indicates why one group might have read the future of their own struggle for civil rights in the success or failure of the other group.[38]

"Unnatural Union"

Placing Cora's history as the descendant of slaves in the midst of Native American conflict, Cooper distinguishes whiteness, defining it by delineating and differentiating black and red identities. The construction of this dissimilarity between black and red also distinguishes slavery and removal, painting each as practices compelled by the essential temperament of these two peoples. Cora's slave ancestry is revealed suggestively at the literal center of the novel, between the two major narrative sequences that divide the book. In the novel's first half, Cora and her sister Alice, with the assistance of young officer Heyward, travel during the French and Indian Wars to meet their father, Munro, a colonel of the British army. Magua, a Native American warrior who seeks to avenge himself against their father, pursues the girls. Natty and his Native American companions Chingachook and Uncas join the party, ensuring that the girls arrive safely at their father's fort. In the novel's second half, Munro surrenders his fort to the French army, and Native Americans who have been fighting alongside the French soldiers attack the already surrendered British forces and their families as they leave the fort. In the melee that ensues, Magua abducts Cora and Alice. A search party that includes Heyward, Natty, Chingachook, and Uncas tracks them, but after they locate the girls, the Delawares capture them all. Their chief, Tamenund decides to release the entire party, but he also concludes that Cora is the legitimate prisoner of Magua, allowing him to flee with her. The party pursues the two, and a battle between Magua and Uncas follows. Cora and Uncas are both killed during this confrontation. Finally, Natty shoots and kills Magua.

Cora's ancestry is revealed prior to the scene in which the English army is massacred by Indians. The details of Cora's origin are revealed when Heyward arrives to deliver a message from Montcalm, but encouraged by Munro, Heyward instead begins to announce his desire to marry Alice. Her father presumes that Heyward has rejected Cora because of her ancestry and chosen his younger daughter, the pale blue-eyed Alice, instead. Believing that Heyward has absorbed the prejudices of the southern United States where he was born, Munro wrathfully defends the worthiness of his darker daughter. When Heyward informs him that he is unaware of her history, Munro explains that Cora's mother was the daughter of a gentleman and lady who were "descended, remotely, from that unfortunate class who are so basely enslaved."[39] He reveals that he met the white British mother of his other daughter, Alice, before he met Cora's mother, but because of his poverty and other reasons, which he does not disclose, her father refused to allow them to marry. After relocating to the West Indies, he became involved with Cora's mother.[40] After her death, he returned to England and married Alice's then-aged mother, "the suffering angel" who had remained celibate since his departure.[41] When Munro confirms that Alice is white, Heyward is relieved. In the scene that follows, Munro abruptly returns to the issue of negotiations with the opposing French general, Montcalm. The two men meet with the general, who informs them that their superior from whom they had requested reinforcements has sent a letter which the French army intercepted informing them that there would be no reinforcements and that they must surrender the fort. When they leave the fort, the soldiers and their families are attacked by 2,000 Hurons.

While the placement of this scene at the novel's center suggests the twin importance of slavery and removal, the novel's transition from the story of Cora's birth to the portrayal of Native Americans as a volatile military force that victimizes unarmed whites also differentiates these issues. This shift suggests both a justification of violence against Native Americans and the impossibility of confronting American slavery within the same context of violence as a defense of civilization. Indeed, because the revelation of Cora's ancestry is initiated by her father's desire to protect his child from racial prejudice, the scene presents those of African descent as dependent and in need of paternal protection. Although slavery emerges in this scene, it remains buried in a remote past, distinct from the pressing issue of Native American conflict to which the novel quickly returns. The most telling elements in this scene are not what Munro says of his affair with Cora's mother but rather what he does not say. Cooper inserts slavery, but he buries the complicated vulnerabilities, painful compromises, and violent encounters that it entailed within the gaps of the past. The language in which Munro couches his relationship with the descendent of the "unfortunate class" is so nebulous that the nature of the relationship remains unclear. He never says that he pursued and married Cora's mother; instead, he says, "[I]t was my lot to form a connection with one who in time became my wife."[42] In addition, as Leslie Fiedler has noted, Munro never uses the words "black" or "Negro."[43] Most important, although Munro says that she eventually became his wife, he does not say whether or not Cora's mother was a slave, or perhaps his slave. The missing details of the social position of Cora's mother obscure the power structure of their relationship, particularly her sexual vulnerability to Munro. Indeed, the susceptibility of Cora and her mother to sexual exploitation have to be inferred from Munro's paranoia that a white man has rejected a marriage to Cora because of her racial heritage. These absences in Cora's history suggest Cooper's attempt to disassociate slavery from the American frontier.

That Cora's origins must be carefully defined suggests the crucial necessity of locating slavery and African ancestry geographically, ethically, and biologically. Cora is the only character in the novel whose source must be defined in a land of immigrants. Cora is read through the lens of the past, her every act before and after this revelation interpreted or reinterpreted through the guise of history. Delineated by the color line, not only does she stand apart from the other characters, but her blackness also limns out their whiteness, their Americanness. As Toni Morrison points out, "It is no accident and no mistake that immigrant populations (and much immigrant literature) understood their 'Americaness' as an opposition to the resident black population."[44] Cora's difference, her blackness, becomes the gauge for Americanness in the novel.

Ultimately, Cora, the faint representation of African presence in the Americas, bears the burden of the past, allowing for the cultural amnesia that the text's expansionist ideology relies on. While Cora's narrative past serves to locate, name, and exclude her from whiteness, the details of her history are suppressed and isolated from the novel's larger narrative. The claim to American lands is sustained by the displacement and suppression of the history of slavery. Cora is the repository for the past that Natty, and by extension Americans, must avoid. While Natty remains the American Adam figure, "an individual emancipated from history, happily bereft of ancestry, untouched and undefiled by the usual inheritances of family and race,"[45] Cora, the miscegenated figure, bears the weight of past sins that the innocent Adam figure escapes. Overdetermined by a complicated racial, colonial, and institutional past, Cora is the personification of history, heredity, family, and race. If, as Donald Pease has pointed out, Natty's denial of this past allows Cooper to "nationalize his identity" and thus "treat Hawkeye's act of taking possession of himself in the woods as a rationale for America's legal title to the frontier," then the historical past that Cora contains allows for that claim.[46]

Cora and the lingering evidence of her racial past indicate the ways in which history precludes the present, the moment in which the American Adam figure must safely reside. Indeed, Cora's convoluted past doubly demands Natty's chronic avowal of his whiteness, his status as a man "without a cross" of nonwhite blood. Natty must remain uncontaminated by the cultural confrontations of the new world, while Cora, who exists because of those cultural confrontations, contains the ever-present possibility of contamination the New World presents. As a figure stained by slavery, colonial acquisition, and miscegenation, Cora possesses a counternarrative to the Adamic narrative, standing in direct conflict with the national identity that the text otherwise embraces. Cora's story embodies the contradiction of slavery in Eden while also rationalizing it as the result of imperialist influences that engender the importation of Africans and the resulting intermixing between people of different continents. Such a darkening of the nation represented for many the failure of this new Eden; they saw miscegenation as the original sin.[47] But in Cooper's narrative, the wages of sin belong to Cora. This representation of Cora exposes what is implicit in the myth of the American Adam: that to be free of ancestry is equivalent to whiteness.[48] Cora exemplifies the dangers of crossing boundaries, not only those of past and present but also those of race and nation. Her racial history confronts the intersections between national histories. Cora represents the "unnatural union" that Munro outlines, a union based on the greed of one nation and the oppression of the other. The "original sin" that Cora bears in this new Eden is not just miscegenation, but the collision of cultures and worlds that Munro says are supposed to remain separate.

Notions and Nations

Ultimately, the narrative of Cora's descent situates slavery as the legacy of Europe. Cora's existence is initiated by aristocratic values that deny Munro his first choice of a fair-haired, blue-eyed wife, thus leading him to a dark woman of the West Indies. Cora's history deflects American responsibility for slavery, casting the institution as the fault of British aristocrats. Munro's story of Cora's birth begins with the greed of the British upper classes. His explanation implies that refusing him permission to marry Alice's mother and permitting him to attach himself to Cora's mother are both the result of the avarice of British fathers, both of whom attempt to sell their daughters to the highest bidders. The aristocratic principles of the British wealthy class prevent his marriage to a white woman, while imperialism makes a woman of African descent available to him. Munro characterizes slavery as "a curse entailed on Scotland by her unnatural union with a foreign and trading people," situating European imperialism as the origin of slavery in the Americas.[49] Ultimately, this deflection attempts to solve the central contradiction of both slavery in the American Eden and racism in the American frontier, where men without pasts, without ancestry, could theoretically build new lives free of aristocratic values. Like Cooper's attempts to distinguish the American spirit from the European one by juxtaposing Natty's rugged sense of justice with European rigidity, Cooper's narrative serves to pose Europe as a rigid hierarchy that spawned slavery while positioning America as an improvisational receptacle of European progeny. The miscegenated figure becomes a way of situating American slavery as an institution reluctantly inherited from Europe, and the narrative returns to the seemingly more immediate problem of Native American conflict.

This framework, which aligns slavery with European imperialism while positing conflict between whites and Indians as the definitive American experience, also emerges in Cooper's *The Travelling Bachelor; or, Notions of the Americans* (1826), a series of essays on the United States written from the perspective of a European man. Despite the shift in genre between *The Last of the Mohicans* and *The Travelling Bachelor,* an examination of the two offers revealing similarities that illuminate the carefully constructed delineation of Cora's past. In *The Travelling Bachelor,* Cooper raises the issues of slavery and Native American removal together, discussing American slavery in a section that is directly followed by an essay on Native Americans. The narrative persona not only equates slavery with the lowest branch of the European class system but also indicts Europe for its involvement in American slavery:

> Is it not a fact that the policy of all America was for more than a century controlled by Europe, and was not this scourge introduced under that policy? . . . It is absurd for France, or for England, to say, we have no slaves in our respective kingdoms, properly so called when everybody knows that the one is at this moment filled with white beggars, and the other with paupers

> who are supported by the public purse. . . . It is true, that two centuries ago, when they had more room, they did not import Negroes from Guinea; but it is, also, just as true, that they sent their ships to convey them to colonies which are situated in climates where they might repay them for their trouble. It is as puerile as it is unjust, therefore, for these two countries, (most others might be included,) to pretend to any exclusive exemption from the sin or shame of slavery.[50]

The text characterizes European greed as the source of the American problem, arguing that Americans, many of whom "have no present agency in [slavery's] existence" and "would gladly be rid of [slavery]," have been burdened with the consequences of European colonization.[51] But in equating European class systems with the American racial system, the text suggests that slavery is an extension of the European social hierarchy and implies that Europe is party to two wrongs—the exploitation of the poor and the exploitation of those of African descent.

Like *The Last of the Mohicans, The Travelling Bachelor* shifts from slavery to the removal of Native Americans, which the narrator describes as the "next subject of interest after the unfortunate descendants of the Africans."[52] While this construction of slavery and Native American removal suggests Cooper's recognition of their interdependence, this section also attempts to differentiate and disengage them. Paralleling the shift in *The Last of the Mohicans* from Cora's slave ancestry to Native American violence, *The Travelling Bachelor* shifts from the representation of blacks as a manageable subordinate to the representation of Native peoples as a potentially aggressive state. *The Travelling Bachelor* represents black slaves as both the leftover fruits of European greed and an inferior body incapable of organized resistance and requiring paternal guardianship and protection, in much the same way that Cora is represented in *The Last of the Mohicans.* Packed with statistics on black-to-white ratios in the slave states, this section opens by arguing that black slaves are not represented in the numbers required to produce a military force, adding that even if they were, they are not competent enough to overpower white men. The text contends that blacks are unequal to the responsibilities of political equality and thus must have their interest represented by white men. In contrast, *The Travelling Bachelor* laments the demise of Native peoples at the same time that it justifies the annihilation of them. The narrator argues that Native peoples should be preserved while also insisting that they were never slain outside of battle. Maintaining that "neither the United States, nor any individual State, has ever taken possession of any land that, by usage or construction might be decreed the property of the Indians, without a treaty and a purchase," he implies that they were slain because of their own aggression toward whites, despite government assistance.[53]

Although Cooper introduces the issues as connected, contending that both blacks and Native peoples "disappear before the superior moral and physical influence of the white," both *The Travelling Bachelor* and *The Last of the Mohicans* distinguish the two, negating the implications of slavery for Native American removal and the implications of Native American removal for slavery.[54] By shaping blacks as unfortunate victims of European avarice and Natives as a military rival to be contended with, both books undo the ways in which slavery and removal together profited settlers. In addition, by casting slaves as the result of a European problem foisted onto Americans, Cooper in effect negates how slavery sustained expansionism by providing labor to work the land and how Native American removal fueled the need for the expansion of slavery.

Cooper's differentiation of Native Americans and African Americans in both *The Travelling Bachelor* and *The Last of the Mohicans* depends on larger cultural constructions of Native American and African-American identities. Winthrop Jordan has noted that because African Americans were not represented in large enough numbers to form a military force in early America and were not recognized as having a national identity, blacks were viewed as a governable "sub-nation" while Native Americans were considered an "ungovernable individuality."[55] Cultural conceptions of Native Americans and African Americans reflect this disparity:

> The Indian became for the Americans a symbol of American experience; it was no mere luck of the toss that placed the profile of an American Indian rather than an American Negro on the famous old five cent piece. Conquering the Indian symbolized and personified the conquest of the American difficulties, the surmounting of the wilderness. To push back the Indian was to prove the worth of one's own mission to make straight in the desert a highway for civilization. With the Negro it was utterly different.[56]

While this distinction defined a space within which to publicly view violence against Native Americans as a valid war against a viable combatant, it also promoted the view of Native Americans as essential to the narrative of American experience. In his study of the regenerative powers attributed to violence in American ideology, Richard Slotkin points out that stories of war with Native Americans expressed a unique American experience and exalted the heroism of whites.[57] Diminishing Native American populations could also be presented as a cultural loss for Americans. The ambivalence of Cooper's treatment of Native American removal expresses this conflict between the ways in which the American experience requires at once the annihilation of Native peoples and the presence of those peoples.

Cooper's depiction of Cora's domestication, in comparison to his representation of Native Americans as ruthless brutes, also reflects the racial ideology of the 1820s and 1830s that asserted that blacks were improved by contact with whites, and that thus slavery was beneficial, while Native Americans in contact with whites only clung more desperately to savagery. Robert Young argues that in an effort to both prove the beneficence of slavery and support the removal of Native Americans, slaveholders represented blacks as accommodating while casting Native Americans as resistant to white society.[58] Cora's rather seamless integration into Munro's European family unit as the caretaker of Alice in the absence of her mother illustrates this theory of black accommodation. Cora also demonstrates her malleability as she shifts from the parlor to the challenges of the frontier with relative ease in comparison to her sister. In contrast, the Native American characters, good and bad, are represented as immune to the supposedly civilizing influence of Europeans. When the travel party of Natty, Heyward, the sisters, Chingachook, and Uncas comes across a young French soldier, Heyward poses as a Frenchman, thus avoiding conflict. Even under those circumstances, Chingachook steals away from the party, kills the soldier, and attaches the scalp to his girdle. Natty deems the attack "a cruel and unhuman act for a white skin," but concedes that "'tis the gift and natur' of an Indian."[59] Though Heyward and Natty disapprove of the act and end their discussion of it to make sure that the women remain unaware of the killing, there is no mention of any reaction from Uncas. Chingachook displays pride in his deed. Not only is he unaffected by the criticism of the white men, he remains unconscious of their displeasure, suggesting that he is incapable of comprehending any interpretation of his act as something other than an honorable achievement.

This dichotomy of conformist blacks and resistant Indians was not unique to Cooper. The conclusion of William Gilmore Simms's *The Yemassee* illustrates this juxtaposition, when Hector, the faithful slave who has just saved his master's life in combat with the Coosaw chief, is granted his freedom and refuses it, saying to his master, "You want Hector for eat acorn wid de hog, and take de swamp wid de Injin, enty?"[60] Horrified by the idea of living like the Indians, Hector proceeds to convince his master that he does not want his liberty. The juxtaposition between the slave who faithfully fights for his master and Native American enemies who resist the encroachment of white settlers suggests that blacks were somehow more adaptable than Native Americans.[61] In *Democracy in America,* Alexis de Tocqueville espoused this theory as well:

> The Negro makes a thousand fruitless efforts to insinuate himself among men who repulse him; he conforms to the taste of his oppressors; while the Indian on the contrary has his imagination inflated with the pretended nobility of his origin. . . . Far from desiring to conform his habits to ours, he loves his savage life as the distinguishing mark of his race and repels every advance to civilization.[62]

To illustrate his point, Tocqueville relays a description of a scene he claims to have witnessed between a black woman, a Native American woman, and a white child sitting in the woods. While the Native American woman, clad in traditional garments, openly caresses the child with an air of "freedom and pride," the black woman, dressed in "squalid European garments . . . endeavored by various little artifices, to attract the attention" of the child in a manner that suggested both "affection for the child and servile fear."[63] Like those who supported removal, Cooper's narrator suggests that while Indians would be susceptible to vice, they would not conform to the cultural values of whites.

Casting Native Americans as tied to the past, incapable of adapting to the present or future, also posed removal as a benevolent act that would both save and civilize Indians. As J. Leitch Wright has pointed out, proponents of removal in the 1820s argued the conflicted theory that separation from whites was the only way to assimilate Indians. If Natives remained on their lands, they would be corrupted by the settlers' worst vices, such as gambling, venereal disease, and alcohol consumption. Despite this susceptibility to the moral depravity of settlers, supporters of removal also argued that Native Americans would not be influenced by the more imitable customs of the settlers. Relocation would protect Indians from these vices, allowing the process of civilization to succeed. As J. Leitch Wright has pointed out, the argument that separation from whites was the only way to assimilate Indians became increasingly prevalent in the 1820s.[64] Cooper's *The Travelling Bachelor* expresses such sentiments, stating that "those who linger near the graves of their fathers . . . become victims to the abuses of civilization, without ever attaining to any of its moral elevation."[65] Like removal supporters, Cooper's narrator suggests that while Indians would be susceptible to vice, they would not conform to the cultural values of whites. Thomas Jefferson's 1818 representation of Native Americans also portrays them as crippled by their allegiance to the past:

> And what chains them to their present state of barbarism and wretchedness, but a bigoted veneration for the supposed superlative wisdom of their fathers, and a preposterous idea that they are to look backward for better things, and not forward longing as it should seem to return to the days of eating acorns and roots rather than indulge in the degeneracies of civilization.[66]

Earlier, in his *Notes on the State of Virginia,* Jefferson had written that Native Americans "astonish you with strokes of the most sublime oratory, such as prove their reason and sentiment strong, their imagination glowing and elevated."[67] Robert Young argues that this disparity between Jefferson's comments represents a dramatic shift in white thought in the early nineteenth century as a result of the threat that Native Americans posed to the social order, particularly because of the flight of slaves into Native American territories.[68]

This formula of compliant blacks and irrationally confrontational Indians functioned as a justification for both slavery and Native American removal; the dichotomy performed as a denial of the inevitability of slave rebellion. Though many planters believed that without supervision slaves might revolt, they generally remained convinced that slaves, with thorough correction, could be reformed.[69] These views suggest that slavery was necessary to provide such correction. The notion that Indians were simply uncorrectable indicated that aggression was an inherent characteristic of Indians rather than a response to white encroachment on their lands. It also pointed to removal as the only viable solution to conflict with Native Americans who were resistant to change, even those changes that were supposedly beneficial. Dichotomizing blacks and Indians worked against looking at these issues as part of a national problem with the treatment of all people who were not white. In other words, representing blacks and Indians as essentially different posed removal and slavery as unrelated issues. This differentiation was particularly important; without it, the stark contradictions between the justification for removing one group of people only to import another group would become obvious.

Aligning the narrative of slavery alongside that of removal raised larger questions about national policy. Only one of these narratives was useful in the construction of an American narrative. Confrontations with Native American populations could be dressed in the trappings of nationalism, but American slavery offered a naked portrait of the dispossessed that was disconnected from the supposed honor of battle. The representation of frontiersmen and Indians, and later cowboys and Indians, was framed by a belief in the righteousness of combat among men, while slavery was the stealing of men, women, and children—not war, but theft. Indeed, connecting Native American removal with race slavery would unravel the guise of American nationalism, exposing lust, greed, and consumption as the underpinning of expansion. The defensive military tactics of Indians could be misconstrued as savage violence that deserved reprisal, but the enslavement of African Americans was far more difficult to incorporate within this narrative. Though it was a given to many that the road to civilization would be paved with the bodies of natives who supposedly stood between whites and their dream of civilizing America, the bodies of African slaves did not fit quite so neatly into this narrative.

"These he said should be slaves"

Though Cooper's portrayal of Cora suggests that the pressing issues of the nation's conflict over slavery did not escape him, slavery remains in the novel's background, occasionally creeping from behind the shadow of conflict between whites and Native Americans.[70] Cooper never depicts slavery; instead, he depicts its product, Cora. Just as Cora remains behind a veil when she is introduced in the novel, the history of slavery is present and yet concealed within Cooper's portrayal of a veiled dark lady with a mysterious history. Cooper includes just one scene which addresses African Americans and Native Americans together. Magua, rather than Cora, delivers this speech. Seeking permission to retain Cora as his prisoner, Magua addresses a speech to Chief Tamenund. Magua begins by delineating the traits of black, white, and red peoples:

> The Spirit that made men colored them differently. . . . Some are blacker than the sluggish bear. These he said should be slaves; and he ordered them to work forever like the beaver. You may hear them groan, when the south wind blows, louder than the lowing buffaloes, along the shores of the great salt lake, where the big canoes come and go with them in droves. Some he made with faces paler than the ermine of the forests: and these he ordered to be traders; dogs to their women, and wolves to their slaves. He gave this people the nature of the pigeon; wings that never tire: young, more plentiful than the leaves on the trees, and appetites to devour the earth. He gave them tongues like the false call of the wildcat; hearts like rabbits; the cunning of the hog (but none of the fox), and arms longer than the legs of the moose. With his tongue, he stops the ears of the Indians; his heart teaches him to pay warriors to fight his battles; his cunning tells him how to get together the goods of the earth; and his arms inclose the land from the shores

> of the salt water to the islands of the great lake. His gluttony makes him sick. God gave him enough and yet he wants all. . . . Some the Great Spirit made with skins brighter and redder than yonder sun . . . and these did he fashion to his own mind. He gave them this island as he had made it, covered with trees, and filled with game. The wind made their clearings; the sun and rains ripened their fruits; and the snows came to tell them to be thankful. What need had they of roads to journey by! They saw through the hills! When the beavers worked, they lay in the shade and looked on. The winds cooled them in summer; in winter, skins kept them warm. If they fought among themselves, it was to prove that they were men. They were brave; they were just; they were happy.[71]

Magua's speech seems only tangentially related to his cause. Considering that neither he nor most of his audience knows that Cora is of African descent, Magua's delineation of the races, particularly his description of the African Americans, appears remote from his quest to maintain possession of Cora. Instead, the speech seems more concerned with reinstating the reliability of racial categories in the United States. Magdalene Mayer has noted that by having a Native American character offer this scheme of racial hierarchy, Cooper implies that it is innate rather than a Western construction.[72] I would add that by having a Native American character not only state this hierarchy but distance the plight of Native Americans from that of African Americans, Cooper reinscribes the distinction between slavery and removal. In Magua's triangular diagram, Africans and Native Americans maintain opposite poles. Magua's speech positions slavery as elsewhere, something heard when the "south wind blows," a ghostly traveling phenomenon. Always coming and going, slavery is associated with no one place, and thus there is no firm accountability for it. Though slaves are represented as subjugated by whites while Native Americans are deceived by them, Magua's framing of this construction as the design of God absolves whites of all responsibility, excusing both slavery and the appropriation of Native American lands. Magua's catalogue is concerned with distinguishing between the races and with using that distinction to justify the treatment of those races. Evoking the "sluggish bear" in his description of the slaves, Magua cast them as an indolent, though manageable, population, requiring white supervision to assume their natural role as laborers. In contrast, he poses Native American resistance as independent of white encroachment on Native lands. Indeed, his description of the Native peoples' peculiar advantages of plentifulness, strength, and bravery positions Native Americans as gifted foes who would fight against each other, if not against whites.

Cora, the sign of slavery, never openly broaches the topic of slavery. Her encounter with Chief Tamenund, however, reveals the complexity of her racialized marginality. After Magua's speech, Cora kneels before Chief Tamenund, begging him to release her and the other captives. When he appears unconvinced, Cora reduces her plea to one for freedom for her sister Alice:

> For myself I ask nothing. Like thee and thine, venerable chief . . . the curse of my ancestors has fallen heavily on their child. But yonder is one who has never known the weight of Heaven's displeasure. . . . She has many, very many, to love and delight in her; and she is too good, much too precious, to become the victim of that villain.[73]

Though the passage reads as a reference to her connection to Munro and his bitter dispute with Magua, which has led to their capture, her designation of her ancestors (not her sister's antecedents) exposes her condition as a racial exile. Her self-deprecating address acknowledges the lack of worth of her own life in comparison to that of her white sister's, and thus she recognizes her failure to fulfill the expectations of white womanhood. Indeed, the distinction between Cora's sturdiness and her sister's frailty acts as a mark of Cora's racial difference. The correlation that Cora draws between Alice's fairness and her virtue acknowledges Cora's unworthiness as the progenitor of American settlers on the frontier: "She is kind, gentle, sweet, good, as mortal may be. There is not a blemish in mind or person at which the proudest of you all would sicken. She is fair—Oh! how surpassingly fair!"[74] In her praise of Alice, Cora implies an association between her own darker skin and dishonor and corruption. By depicting Cora's submission to dominant cultural interpretations of race, Cooper's narrative supports the representation of those of African descent as cultural conformists without any coherent cultural codes of their own.

Cora's difference from Native Americans is also indicated in her exchange with Chief Tamenund. Indeed, Tamenund's response to Cora's pleadings—"What art thou?"—conveys Cora's double alienation from the Native peoples and the whites in the novel.[75] Cora's reply, "A woman. One of a hated race, if thou wilt—a Yengee," suggests that an inability to name her racially determines the chief's use of "what," rather than "who." Though she finally identifies herself as a "Yengee," a term Cooper's Native Americans apply to whites, her delineation of her origins and the abrupt and perhaps cautious insertion of "Yengee" serves as a reminder of Cora's liminal status. When Tamenund remarks that white men would refuse to marry a woman "whose blood was not of the color of snow,"[76] Cora is crushed with shame, and the audience is reminded that concubinage to a white man is a likely outcome for her. By defining Cora against Alice and separating her from the Native American women in the texts, Cooper prepares the way for Cora's death. He excises the miscegenated figure, and thus the mark of slavery, from the novel with one fatal wound, leaving conflict between whites and Native Americans to be represented by the final encounter between Natty and Magua; the story resumes without her.

By foregrounding issues concerning Indian removal in *The Last of the Mohicans,* Cooper retreats from the moral conflict that slavery poses, reflecting a cultural inability to confront the inevitable contradictions that American slavery offered to a nation that supposedly symbolized liberty. Just as Crèvecoeur had earlier praised the tenets of American liberty and addressed American slavery in a separate chapter in his *Letters from an American Farmer,* Cooper attempts to contain slavery in history; within the temporal space of the novel, it produces a counternarrative. With its exposition of the problems that Native American removal posed and its repression of the contradictions that African-American slavery presented, *The Last of the Mohicans* is an example of a pattern that characterized American responses to these two issues. Richard Drinnon has noted that while the writers of the Declaration of Independence consciously omitted the mention of American slavery, in that same document they also explicitly referred to Native Americans as "merciless Indian savages."[77] This avowal of the savagery of Native Americans and exclusion of African Americans points to a fundamental difference in how the two groups were conceived of in the American imagination, a difference that emerges in *The Last of the Mohicans* through the explicit confrontation with violence against Native Americans and the implicit references to slavery through the treatment of Cora.

2

A Land without Names: National Anxiety in *The Slave; or, Memoirs of Archy Moore*

In a letter addressed to *The Liberator,* antislavery activist and author Lydia Maria Child wrote of Richard Hildreth's antislavery novel *The Slave; or, Memoirs of Archy Moore* (1836): "If I were a man, I would rather be the author of that work, than anything ever published in America."[1] It is ironic that the book almost remained unpublished in America. According to Hildreth, he could not find a publisher for his novel and had to print the book at his own expense. Still, no bookseller would put his name on the title page of the book. Though Hildreth later complained that only a personal friend "had the courage . . . to insert his own name in the imprint," Hildreth himself published the book anonymously.[2] Early reviews of the novel suggest that perhaps the reluctance of publishers and booksellers was warranted. John O. Sargent of *The Atlas* wrote of the book:

> Some of its details are of a character too revolting to be made public. . . . Were it not for a few passages which we could hardly attribute to a female pen, we might suppose it the production of a lady. . . . But it appears to be the work of a man—and a man of singular strength and power of mind. . . . We are aware of no purpose [that such books] can answer, save that of sustaining and impelling a dangerous excitement.[3]

Others offered harsher criticisms. In the *Boston Daily Advocate,* one critic contended that the printer should be banned from printing and perhaps hung unless he revealed the author of the book, who could then be hung in his stead.[4]

Though there were those, like Child, who praised the novel for its truth-telling, one need look no further than the plot for the source of the controversy surrounding the novel. The central character, Archy, the nearly white son of a mixed-race slave and her master, initiates a love affair with his half-sister Cassy, another nearly white mixed-race slave. Though he knows that she is his half-sister, Archy decides to marry Cassy, who has no idea that Archy is her brother. When their father, Master Moore, finds out, he is incensed, not because they are half-siblings but because he wants Cassy, his daughter, as a mistress for himself. Despite the opposition of their master/father, Archy and Cassy declare themselves married and ask God's sanction. Realizing that Moore will punish them harshly, they run away together, but they are soon captured and reprimanded. Archy is sold away, and Cassy is placed in a cottage to be her father's lover. Again she escapes, but she is held captive by a poor white couple. Eventually she is sold to a kind widow, who miraculously lives in the same neighborhood as Archy, and the two are reunited. Archy and Cassy live happily together for a year and have a son. But Archy's new master is in debt, and Archy is sold once again. Finding himself in the power of a harsh overseer, Archy again runs away, and after a lengthy hiatus in the wilderness, he makes his way north by passing as white. He becomes a sailor and eventually settles in England as a wealthy man, vowing to find his wife and son.

Considered the first antislavery novel, the text is teeming with portrayals and themes that would long be a part of both antislavery fiction and mulatto fiction written during the nineteenth and twentieth centuries. The book has been called a model for Stowe's *Uncle Tom's Cabin.*[5] Indeed, Archy has been described as "a proto–Joe Christmas," because of his self-conscious awareness that his heritage has isolated him from others.[6] Both Archy and Cassy reveal the seeds of gendered portrayals of mixed-raced figures. Archy displays both the cowardice of mixed-race characters such as Clarence of *The Garies and Their Friends* and Honoré f.m.c. of *The Grandissimes* and the heroism of George of *Uncle Tom's Cabin* or Louis of *Minnie's Sacrifice.* Cassy foreshadows mulatto characters driven to attempt daring escapes, such as Eliza's famous trek across the ice. In addition, though the way in which Archy's life is conscribed by illicit sex was the source of the controversy about the book, sexual indiscretion would become a common topic of mixed-race literature. Antislavery propaganda was filled with stories of sexually abused female mulatto figures, and much later mulatto fiction was fixated on sexual exploitation. In addition, women writers such as Lydia Maria Child and Harriet Beecher Stowe would incorporate tales of sexual abuse in their works. But as the first antislavery novel, Hildreth's lengthy story of sexual abuse compounded by incest and violence left even some antislavery organizations uncomfortable with the book.[7]

The incubation of mulatto fiction within the antislavery agenda contributed to a web of sexual excess that drapes many of these figures. Clearly, the sexual implications of mulatto figures had a particular resonance within antislavery propaganda. Jules Zanger has noted "the very existence of the octoroon convicted the slaveholder of prostituting his slaves and of selling his own children for profit."[8] Certainly antislavery advocates exploited this significance. However, the recurring instances of sexualized violence in *Archy Moore* suggest a habitual anxiety that points to larger themes within the antislavery movement, particularly its emphasis on the dangers of human tyranny and the need for personal restraint. During the rise of the antislavery movement of the 1830s, this focus on the need to restrain inner passions, especially sexual impulses, coincided with rapid social change and increasingly ill-defined class distinctions.[9] Mulatto characters, the physical manifestation of the breaking of sexual taboos, allowed writers to project their fears of a nation out of control and to engage in titillating fantasies of the same origin. By framing mulatto figures within this scheme of sexual indulgence, Hildreth expressed this anxiety about the American condition while also exploring the sexual implications of a world without restraint.

When Hildreth, a professed abolitionist, published this novel in 1836, the abolitionist movement had already begun to gain direction and strength. As the movement took shape, abolitionists exhibited a deep concern for the relationship between absolute power and total submission; antislavery rhetoric and literature included frequent references to the evils of tyranny and unguarded passion. According to Ronald Walters, for some abolitionists, the problem with slavery was not merely cruelty but rather the imbalance of power inherent in the institution. This inequity often led to a lack of restraint on the part of the empowered. While slavery epitomized this principle, many abolitionists did not attribute this desire to tyrannize solely to southern slaveholders. Instead, many viewed these social problems as the result of a desire for power inherent in all men; thus, what was happening in the South could happen anywhere. The South was merely one example of what could happen when men's basest passions were allowed to dominate.[10]

Many of the efforts of abolitionists to quell these inner passions focused on human sexuality. As Walters asserts, in the 1830s, power was beginning to imply "human sexuality as the deepest, most mysterious, most fearful force of all."[11] To many abolitionists, there was little difference between lust for power and sheer lust. According to Peter Walker, for some abolitionists, sex became a metaphor for an America in a state of "wild delirium."[12] It is no surprise that other movements that abolitionists involved themselves in had sexually charged implications that centered on the need to control the appetites. Causes such as anti-prostitution, temperance campaigns, and even warnings against masturbation attracted many abolitionists.[13]

Abolitionists were not the only ones among whom this concern with social restraint developed. Warnings against the dangers of sexual intercourse increased in medical literature during the 1830s. According to historian Charles Rosenberg, control was considered by many to be the "basic building block of personality," and many agreed that men were controlled by their fondness for domination. Uncontrolled sexuality was viewed as a sign of the degeneration of civilization.[14] Walker argues that while previous generations had been concerned with social control and tyranny, the obsession with the necessity of human restraint in the 1830s was a residual effect of social change as a result of western exploration, massive land acquisitions, increasing immigration, and industrialization. From these circumstances came the "emergence of democratic man, who was likewise a marginal man without roots, prescriptively defined purpose, and the comforting sense of place in the world and its affairs."[15] Rosenberg adds that much of this need to restrain the passions of men stemmed from the fact that class was particularly ill-defined at the time. The framing of restraint and virtue as middle-class values may have assuaged class anxiety:

> [T]he repression of sexuality could mean security, the ability to predict economic and social reality—in short, autonomy and social respectability—in a period when the urban lower and lower-middle classes had few enough areas for the establishment of ego function. . . . [T]he very process of deferring pleasure . . . provided one mode through which individuals of marginal social status might begin to find security and dignity.[16]

The emphasis on the need for restraint in antislavery rhetoric and fiction reflects this underlying anxiety about the state of American society. Indeed, the focus on slavery may have been an attempt to project larger social issues on a single region of the nation. Imagining social upheaval as confined to the South could allow abolitionists to minimize the significance of social problems that riddled the North, such as prostitution, illegitimacy, birth control, and abortion.[17] Focusing on the South could also allow abolitionists to approach social problems in miniature, using the South as a condensed replica. But ultimately, the larger issue of the need for self-control could form a new system of classification to organize what may have seemed like a society unhinged.

Mulatto figures presented a vehicle for exploring the relationship between sexual excess and the loss of social distinctions. They offered compelling shorthand for the effects of miscegenation, prostitution, illegitimacy, and adultery. In addition, they could be used to manipulate the class anxiety beneath the call for restraint. In a culture where class was becoming increasingly elusive as a social marker, race was a particularly important distinction.[18] Mulatto figures represented the ultimate threat, a blurring of social divisions in an already hazy world. They signified the chaos that threatened to endanger civilization. Because the product of miscegenation implied sexual sin, mixed-race figures had special meaning in a nation founded on the principle of a new Eden. If, as Winthrop Jordan has asserted, "a darkened nation would mean that animal sex governed American destiny and that the experiment in the wilderness had failed," then mulatto figures offered the ultimate symbol of the loss of the American Eden.[19] As Mason Stokes has noted in his exploration of nineteenth-century American theological interpretations of the Eden myth, ultimately miscegenation becomes the reason for the fall from paradise.[20] These multiple anxieties that mulatto characters elicited made them rich in meaning for antislavery writers. If their concern had been solely to express the conditions of slavery, then mixed-race figures would not have appeared in the numbers that they did in antislavery propaganda and literature. Toni Morrison argues that in many cases the construction of what she calls the "Africanist presence," or the fabrication of blackness in American literature, is self-reflexive, a meditation on the self.[21] Illustrating this theory, Hildreth's representation of characters of African descent and the institution of slavery suggests an exploration of the nature of the American self, and thus the national character.

A Land without Names

Social anxiety is evident in Hildreth's introduction, which he later appended to the novel. When Hildreth offered his summation of what had inspired his antislavery novel, he began not by discussing his firsthand witnessing of slavery in Florida (where he retired during illness) but with his detailed observations of the whites that he encountered while he was there.[22] He describes the wealthy families from Virginia who "belonged to the highest and best class of southern society," their rivals the South Carolinians, and a "much ruder class, including many specimens of those known as 'Georgia crackers' . . . one section of the great depressed class generally known throughout the south as 'poor white men.'"[23] He also mentions a group that was rather difficult to define; those who were slaveholders, many of whom were from Kentucky, but who apparently were not among the "best class of

Southern society." Hildreth explains that with the exception of the poor whites, all of them had come to Florida with slaves, among whom "diversities were to be observed, narrower indeed in range, but hardly less striking than those existing among their masters."[24]

While it seems odd that in his explanation for the novel's development, Hildreth would include this thorough description of the assortment of immigrants to the state of Florida, his attempt to classify them within the context of an antislavery novel betrays his discomfort with what he saw of the nation's expansion. Certainly Hildreth's description of diversity among the whites suggests that his observation of slavery would be representative rather than confined to a particular region. However, his emphasis on the "diversities" among not only the slaveholders, but also poor whites, and the slaves, reveals his apprehension about the impression of disorderly miscellany that Florida had left with him. His attempt to catalogue the neighborhood demonstrates his need to impose some system of organization that could define this inventory of slaveholders, nonslaveholders, and slaves; wealthy, impoverished, and in between. But in his effort to sort his neighbors, nothing more than a list of American states emerges. Embedded in this apprehension about immigration to a new state is the larger issue of a growing nation composed of immigrants, a place where identity would not be a constant entity but instead could be a shifting self-defined idea.

This anxiety erupts in *The Slave; or, Memoirs of Archy Moore,* where family connections are denied, origins and identity become difficult to delineate, and disastrous consequences result. The narrator initiates the central narrative by explaining that family names had "little weight" in most parts of America.[25] This problem sparks the plot development at the core of the novel, the triangular incestuous relationship between Archy, his sister Cassy, and their father Colonel Moore. In this world where identity and origins can be consciously denied, social codes quickly degenerate and a land run by sexual desire unfolds. Mulatto figures, as the product of extramarital miscegenation, evoke the destruction of the family unit, the supposed foundation for the organization of society. Their undefined status, both racial and familial, threatens to make social codes of classification ineffectual. The incest of the characters in Hildreth's novel embodies an irreversible cycle of social deterioration that once initiated cannot be rectified.

The central dilemma that emerges in the text is not so much slavery but rather the denial of origins that allows men to feed their unquenchable appetite for sexual violation. Just like his father, Archy is able to exploit veiled identities to gratify his own lust. His licentious yearning is portrayed as a natural tendency that goes unchecked. In fact, Archy's incestuous impulses are not limited to Cassy. As Werner Sollors has pointed out, Archy also displays similar urges toward his mother: "I describe her more like a lover than a son. . . . I watched her, almost with a lover's earnestness, while she fondled me on her lap. . . . But I was very far from being her only admirer."[26] Hence, Archy's lustfulness is not the direct result of his enslavement. Instead, the desires that he has harbored since the early stages of childhood fester because of the failure of plantation culture to regulate the behavior of slaves and slaveholders. The placid manner in which Archy describes his incestuous designs toward both women only magnifies the instinctual nature of his attraction. Implicit in the problem of namelessness is the lack of sexual accountability that it permits, not merely for the slaveholder but for the slave as well.

Through Archy's intense ardor toward Cassy, Hildreth demonstrates how this innate passion overwhelms individual discernment. Archy is absorbed by his attraction to Cassy with an "intoxication of passion" that makes him capable of ignoring the abuses of slavery that surround him as long as they do not interfere with his visits to Cassy. Even after Colonel Moore makes his intentions toward Cassy known, Archy remains immersed in his lustful happiness: "The ecstasy of passion still supported me. . . . Be absorbed in any passion, and while the fit continues, you will find yourself endowed with a surprising and almost superhuman energy."[27] This delight in excess that Archy experiences coincides with stints of alcoholism and tyranny over fellow slaves, but sexual impulses directed toward his sister determine the primary course of his life.

By portraying Cassy as a devout Methodist incapable of resisting this corruption, Hildreth brings the cycle of sin in which Archy and Cassy are trapped into focus. Unaware of Archy's identity, Cassy's religious values are ineffectual. Though she has adopted a system of interpreting the world according to religious conviction, the world does not conform to her moral code. She avoids the clutches of Colonel Moore because of her religious values, but those same values also lead her to assume that because Archy wants to marry her, his intentions are honorable. Her binary understanding of morality cannot account for the ambiguous identities that inhabit her world. It is interesting that although everyone else on the plantation seems to know that they are siblings, including their mistress, who arranges their marriage, Cassy never inquires about Archy's father despite the fact that she and Archy are the two fairest slaves on the plantation. Her acceptance of religion and the sanctity of marriage makes her blind to the dangers that surround her, and masked origins become invisible traps that she lacks the information to avoid. Juxtaposing Archy's deviant desire with Cassy's traditional religious beliefs, Hildreth demonstrates how for Cassy sin is inescapable. Indeed, as the physical manifestations of illicit desire, these mixed-race characters by their very existence recall the irredeemable original sin. As Archy says of slavery: "It is impossible to build any edifice of good on so evil a foundation."[28] No religious sacrament can rectify the sanctions already broken. Hildreth describes a world in which religion is inept in the midst of irreparable social confusion.

Because the story is told from Archy's perspective, Colonel Moore's pursuit of Cassy is depicted as the most abominable example of human depravity. In his depiction of the interactions between Cassy and Colonel Moore, Hildreth develops the focal point of his representation of incest—the issue of paternity, or the importance of definitive origins that offer a system of social organization. When Colonel Moore insists that Cassy become his mistress, Cassy utters the words that are her only hope for intervention, saying "Master, —Father . . . what is it you would have of your own daughter?"[29] Hearing these words, Moore freezes and immediately desists. The mere acknowledgment of their relationship temporarily stops even the most violent of passions.

This problem of paternity in a world of namelessness is a reflection of the deep concern for maintaining social order in the form of class and racial distinctions. Without clearly defined and acknowledged links that locate station, relationship, and even racial identity, incest seems inevitable. Incest symbolizes the absence of a well-defined social system. Ann Dalke notes that in early American novels, class anxiety was often represented in the form of incest. Without clear class distinctions, male characters could unknowingly become involved with women of the lower classes who would turn out to be the illegitimate relatives.[30] Oddly, in the case of *Archy Moore,* Colonel Moore and Archy are perfectly aware of their relationship to Cassy. But their profound sexual desires for Cassy inspire them to consciously deny the relationship. In the tangled skein of incestuous relationships that Hildreth creates, aberrant human desire that goes unchecked by social restraints is the origin of social confusion.

The Gothic in *Archy Moore*

The exploration of aberrant sexual desire in the novel oscillates between repulsion and prurient fascination that is often expressed in an intersection between the gothic and the pornographic. According to David Reynolds, some nineteenth-century reform literature displayed a "dialectic of erotic enjoyment followed by recoil and deflection," and antislavery literature was no exception.[31] As slavery became a site to explore violence and sex, abolition, like other reform movements, was threatened by sensationalism and sadistic fantasy. Reynolds traces the expression of such fantasy back to William Lloyd Garrison's first issue of *The Liberator,* arguing that sexually charged portraits of American slaves were intrinsic to the antislavery movement practically from its inception. Even the earliest issues of *The Liberator* contained stories entitled "Burning Alive," "Horrible Butchery!!" and "Blood! Blood! Blood!"[32] These portrayals of a world controlled by sexual desire allowed writers both to explore the effects of social mayhem and to reenact the forbidden.

This intersection between antislavery literature and the pornographic is tied to the abolitionist obsession with absolute power versus total submission, a scenario that often fueled erotic literature during the nineteenth century.[33] Slavery offered another venue to explore the sexual implications of authority versus vulnerability. While abolitionists probably were not attracted to slavery as a social cause because it offered a vehicle to explore this pornographic scenario, the obsession of some abolitionists with this power scheme suggests the possibility of a prurient interest in the sexual implications of slavery. This paradigm embedded in slavery offered a way to explore what Karen Halttunen calls the "pornography of pain," or the spectacle of suffering, which formed the dominant convention of sexual pornography by the early nineteenth century.[34] This eroticization of pain, particularly through images of flagellation in humanitarian reform literature, made slavery especially conducive to eliciting prurient excitement and voyeuristic fantasy.[35] According to Halttunen, reform writers' "treatment of scenarios of suffering, if not narrowly pornographic in nature, assumed that the spectacle of pain was a source of illicit excitement, prurience, and obscenity—the power to evoke revulsion and disgust."[36] Halttunen maintains that to avoid implicating themselves as those who received pleasure from witnessing and recounting these scenarios of pain, reform writers included descriptions of their own emotional responses to suffering. But, according to Halttunen, "the sensitivity to pain to which they thus laid claim proved less a matter of sentimental sympathy than of Gothic horror and revulsion, and disgust."[37]

This mixture of pornographic interest and gothic repulsion is often an element within portrayals of mixed-race figures. As the product, perpetrators, and victims of sexual excess in a world without boundaries, mixed-race characters merge a lengthy list of carnal transgressions and thus offer a salacious gaze at deviant sexuality. If as Steven Marcus argues, pornography exists "to violate in fantasy that which has been tabooed," then the sexualized portrayal of mulatto figures whose very existence depends on a breach of social prohibitions could invite readers to perform the infraction in fantasy.[38] In addition, the ritual sexualized violence and incest that surrounds mulatto figures compounds their eroticization.

The gothic offers a discourse in which to both express anxiety about anarchy that is embedded in the exploration of sexual excess and to deflect the sensual pleasure associated with these depictions. As H. L. Malchow observes, the gothic forms a "language of panic, unreasoning anxiety and distancing sensationalism."[39] Thus, the fear of social disorder in Hildreth's work sometimes erupts in the form of the horrific and repulsive. It is not surprising that fiction involving mixed-race characters often displays the trappings of gothic fiction, such as the return of the repressed, doubles, violence, incest, sinful secrets, rape, and sometimes the supernatural. Various permutations of gothic elements are included in texts from Victor Sejour's "The Mulatto" (1837) to Pauline Hopkins's *Of One Blood* (1903). In antislavery literature in particular, the gothic offered a medium through which to explore "anarchic forces of passion and appetite, carnal lust and blood lust," all of which formed a focal point for antislavery propaganda.[40] As Halttunen has asserted, "[The gothic] treatment of torture closely linked pain with beauty, and cruelty with sexual desire, articulating an erotic sensibility."[41] The gothic provided a way to explore the basest components of human nature while also interjecting the element of horror in an attempt to restrain prurient titillation. The need to deflect the erotic interest in these portrayals only confirms this dark side of human nature; the attempt to deflect ultimately fails and begins this cycle of attraction and deflection again. Nevertheless, the gothic offered a method both to explore and to resist the sexual fantasies that emerge in mixed-race fiction.

This oscillation between attraction and repulsion in *Archy Moore* appears as Hildreth situates the details of sexual excess within a series of gothic elements. Archy's discovery that his master is his father is revealed in the deathbed revelation of his mother. Archy and Cassy's hideaway on the run where they experience sexual freedom is a dilapidated house believed to be haunted. The sexual indulgence of the central characters is always characterized by the horror of incest, and innocence is frequently threatened by seasoned evil. Carefully planted incidents, such as Archy's attempted infanticide of his child born of incest, fill the text with horrific images that infuse titillation with a dose of horror.

Nevertheless, a salacious bent fuels these thrilling portrayals. From the very beginning of *Archy Moore,* the prurient interest in witnessing the pain of others surfaces as the narrator, Archy, offers this invitation: "Ye who would know what evils man can inflict upon his fellow without reluctance, hesitation, or regret; ye who would learn the limit of human endurance, and with what bitter anguish and indignant hate, the heart may swell, and yet not burst, peruse these Memoirs!"[42] He solicits readers to indulge in a voyeuristic exploration of human excess. Indeed, the construction of the text as a memoir adds an element of authenticity to its professed ability to enable readers to gaze upon the "bitter anguish" of others. But the impression of foreboding in the passage's almost biblical forecast of evil also reveals a strand of fearful aversion.

This vacillation between fascination and repulsion also manifests in violent incestuous interactions. In a disturbing portrayal of Moore's violence toward Archy and Cassy, the lines between revulsion and titillation are blurred. Captured after a failed attempt to escape Moore's sexual advances toward Cassy, the two find themselves chained together awaiting their punishment. A drunken Colonel Moore soon arrives, angered that they have not been separated. He has Archy stripped almost naked and hung from the ceiling. Then, in a dramatic scene, he hands Cassy a heavy whip and warns her, "[I]f you wish to save your own carcass, see that you bring blood at every blow."[43] Though she faints at his request, she is revived and again ordered to whip Archy. Refusing, she replies, "Master, he is my husband!" which sends Moore into a paroxysm of rage.[44] He strikes Cassy with his fists and tramples her. He then turns his wrath on Archy, beating him so furiously with the whip that pools of blood lay at his feet. To quiet the screaming Archy, Colonel Moore wedges the butt of another whip into his mouth.

Gerald Early has referred to this scene as a "bizarre gothic picture."[45] Both horrific and yet titillating to audiences, the scene is brimming with Moore's hyperactive sexual desires. But as it mines the depths of Colonel Moore's psyche, the scene blurs the focus on slavery. Clearly the institution of slavery is the site of his debauchery, and yet the details of his sinister lustful violence reduce slavery to a dispensable backdrop, a prism that reveals the human subterrain. As Colonel Moore's sexual attraction shifts between his children, Cassy and Archy, his compounded frustrated desire offers a libidinous spectacle of incestuous homoeroticism. It is Archy who is stripped naked, Archy who is hung from the ceiling, Archy who is beaten profusely, and Archy who has the butt of a whip placed in his mouth. Colonel Moore's desire to emasculate Archy through this bondage scenario with Cassy as dominatrix displays his own furious sadism; the issue of slavery is completely overshadowed by the scene's voyeuristic allure.

The scene illustrates a chaotic world in miniature, driven by mysterious inner passions that defy social convention. The scenario in which Cassy's reference to Archy as "husband" initiates this body tirade illustrates the problem of social confusion. Colonel Moore's resistance to Cassy's attempt to order the situation by naming her relation to Archy dramatizes social order and social anarchy as diametrics in contention. Within this context, the female mulatto's role as the manifestation of sin, despite her own innocence, embodies this tension between disorder and order. Because her desire to give order to the chaos from which she was born is thwarted by the same powerful desires that give her life, the inability to break the cycle of sin that has already been initiated is evident. Doomed to have the sins of her father visited upon her, Cassy's inextricable link to illicit sexual desire cannot be severed.

Indeed, even in her unwitting innocence, Cassy becomes a stick figure in this gothic/pornographic role play. As a vacuous representation of feminine virtue and chastity, her innocence is the dramatic foil to Colonel Moore's evil and therefore enables the performance. The sexual implications of Cassy's powerlessness within this structure are provocative. Even her resistance is obscured by a clinging dependence that reduces her to a performer within this scenario.

> [P]oor child [Cassy]—[she] heard him with shame and horror; and was ready,—she told me,—to sink into the earth, with terror and dismay. In relating it, she blushed—she hesitated—she shuddered—her breathing became short and quick—she clung to me, as if some visible image of horror were present before her;—and, bringing her lips close to my ear, she exclaimed in a trembling and scarcely audible whisper—"Oh Archy!—and he my father!"[46]

Even her innocence, her vulnerability, and her horror, expressed in the soft whispers of quivering lips, are seductive. This impression is compounded by the detailed descriptions of Cassy's near-rape as Colonel Moore "dragged her towards the bed" repeatedly.[47] Hildreth capitalizes on these voyeuristic implications, and any potential protest of the sexual abuse of slave women is devoured by prurience.

Masculinity and "The Pleasure of Pursuit"

In contrast to Hildreth's portrayal of Cassy as a poor innocent, his representation of Archy is complicated by his interpretation of manhood as essentially aggressive. Hildreth represents inner aggression and the gratification of violent passions as dangers to larger society, but he also depicts these characteristics as productive traits of masculine identity. Thus, the necessity for restraint and perpetuation of an aggressive masculine ethos are competing ideas within the novel. Though Archy asserts that "animal appetites are by no means, the only motive of human action," he also says:

> It is the pleasure of pursuit and the struggle, it is the very labor of their attainment, in which consists the happiness they bring. . . . He whom circumstances permit to yield to this impulse of his nature, and to pursue—successfully or not . . . the objects which have captivated his fancy, may be regarded as having all the chance for happiness.[48]

This emphasis on the importance of pursuit validates both Archy's quest for freedom and his manipulative pursuit of Cassy. As Sollors has noted, Hildreth at times nearly endorses Archy's incest with Cassy.[49] Ultimately, this desire for pursuit is closely akin to a competitive longing to dominate others. For Archy, pursuit frequently manifests itself in calculating and even hostile behavior, all of which is portrayed as the expression of a dynamic masculine self. According to Rosenberg, in the early nineteenth century, "[T]he primary role model with which men had to come to terms was that which articulated the archaic male ethos—one in which physical vigor and particularly aggressive sexual behavior was a central component."[50] In adhering to this ideology of masculinity, Hildreth makes Archy as much the perpetrator as he is the victim. He not only dupes Cassy into an incestuous marriage to satisfy his own lust, he also delights in his assumed superiority over darker slaves, drinks heavily, and even tyrannizes over other slaves when he becomes a slave-driver. Though his behavior often mimics that of his masters, he is portrayed as essentially good, though flawed. Colonel Moore's incest is wrong, and yet as Hildreth puts it in the opening "Advertisement" for the novel, "few have better claims to indulgence than Archy Moore." That which is portrayed as abuse of power in white slaveholders becomes a triumph of defiant manhood in a slave.

In this portrayal of Archy as aggressively defiant, his relevance to later mulatto heroes is evident. Yet Archy is both like and unlike later male mulatto figures. He is sometimes courageous, like Stowe's George Harris, but his courage is often fleeting and quickly exchanged for cowardice. While he is like Frank Webb's Clarence of *The Garies and Their Friends* (1857), who betrays signs of physical and emotional weakness and selfish purpose, Archy sometimes demonstrates physical vitality and daring leadership. Hildreth's novel may have influenced many later portrayals of mulatto figures; however, as Nicholas Canaday Jr. has noted, in the portrayal of Archy, Hildreth escapes the confines of stereotyping.[51] Indeed, it would be difficult to argue that any fully formed mulatto stereotype existed when Hildreth wrote the novel. Nevertheless, the inconsistency in Archy's character highlights Hildreth's representation of him as a man who struggles to achieve this idea of self-assertive manhood, demonstrating a more complex configuration than Stowe or Webb's male interracial figures.

It is problematic that the achievement of this manhood is directly linked to harnessing his innate aggression toward others. Archy exhibits the same penchant for domination that the white men in the novel display. Even as a child he learns to dominate his invalid master, who is also his half-brother. Reflecting on the experience, he asserts that he "found little difficulty in maintaining that actual superiority, to which my superior vigor both of body and mind, so justly entitled me."[52] As an adult, this desire for power manifests itself in abusing his authority over the other slaves as a slave-driver. While he does not describe the details of his wrongs against his fellow slaves, he notes that he found power both "dangerous and intoxicating."[53] Discovering that he too has become a tyrant, he concludes that power in the hands of anyone must be checked. Archy laments his behavior, but he is not very remorseful about generalized aggression toward others, although he does regret acts that he perceives as excessive violence against those who are entirely within his power. To achieve the ideal of vigorous manhood, this aggressive predisposition has to be redirected from the trampling of the defenseless to participation in bilateral conflict. Violence must be committed in the spirit of rebellion and revenge to achieve manhood in the novel.

Hildreth introduces Thomas, a slave of "unmixed blood," as the embodiment of the productive attributes of this masculine ethos. Described as being of a fine mind, Thomas initially is the ideal slave. Obedient, hard-working, and content with his lot, he has been raised by Methodists who used religious teachings in "subduing the resistance of the superstitious and trembling slave."[54] According to Archy, Thomas's "passions were strong and even violent; but what is very rare among slaves, he had them completely under his control."[55] Through steady labor and goodwill, Thomas gains the favor of the overseer as well as his fellow slaves. Though Archy has little sympathy with Thomas's religious views, he too admires and befriends him. Nonetheless, when the overseer brutally beats his wife, Thomas undergoes a dramatic transformation. He snatches the whip from the overseer and the overseer nearly shoots him. After appealing to his master, Thomas and his wife are both beaten furiously. Her resulting death marks the triumph of Thomas's innate aggression over his training: "It was plain that natural feeling was fast gaining the mastery over that system of artificial constraint in which [Thomas] had been educated."[56] Thomas soon converts to "certain wild rites" that he had learned from his African mother.[57] He organizes a group of bandits that includes Archy and leads them in pillaging the property of local slaveholders.

Thomas's conversion represents the demarcation between a man and a slave in the context of the novel. This delineation juxtaposes the artificial constraints of society and the intuitive spirit of antagonism as Thomas discards his religious views and releases formerly constrained passions. Hildreth's portrayal of a full black character as the embodiment of rebellion and revenge suggests the image of the primitive savage casting off the veneer of civilization. Hildreth capitalizes on Thomas's African heritage, representing it as the epitome of uncivilized existence. However, as Canaday has pointed out, Thomas is not merely a noble savage figure, in part because of his evolution from capitulation to defiance.[58] Because Hildreth portrays all male characters as teetering on this line between savage impulses and social restraint, Thomas's transition suggests the ascendance of the spirit that lives in all men. The depiction of Thomas as a man who has surrendered to his inner passions becomes another vehicle to explore male indulgence.

Archy's own lack of insubordination is magnified by this portrayal of Thomas, and ultimately Thomas guides Archy's initiation into manhood. At the sight of Thomas's wife being beaten, Archy reflects: "[N]othing but the base and dastard spirit of a slave could have endured that scene of female torture and distress, and not have interfered."[59] Archy's head grows dizzy at the sight of the beating, and though he claims that he longed to seize the overseer, he does nothing. Only Thomas, in whom "the spirit of manhood" had not been extinguished, responds.[60] Thomas's influence over Archy becomes evident when the two run away together and capture the overseer, Martin, who killed Thomas's wife. While Thomas coolly announces that the man must die that night, Archy is horrified at the idea of killing the man. As he puts it, "[T]here still crept about my heart some remains of that slavish fear and servile timidity, which the bolder spirit of Thomas had wholly shaken off."[61] Archy tries to convince Thomas that if they return Martin to the plantation, he will make sure they are pardoned in appreciation. But Thomas calmly maintains that Martin must die that very night. He gives Martin a half hour to repent his sins, and while Archy is dizzy and faint at the thought, Thomas with composure shoots Martin as he pleads for mercy. Proceeding on their journey, Archy is no longer frightened; instead, for the first time he experiences the "lofty feeling of manhood vindicated, and tyranny visited with a just retribution."[62] The murder of Martin marks Archy's initiation into manhood.

This act also launches the men's passage into a life free of social confines. Under the leadership of Thomas, Archy begins to live in the "wild of the woods."[63] With a band of other runaways, Archy and Thomas live in the wilderness, hunt for food, make clothes, and trade with other slaves. This is a space where there are natural outlets for their aggression, and they are allowed to meet foes with equal violence. They engage in vicious fights for their freedom when they encounter slavecatchers. Canaday describes Archy's transition from slavery to this wild landscape thus: "As we see Archy at last gaining a manhood that he will never lose, born in violence and nurtured in what amounts to guerilla warfare for several months before he reaches free soil[,] we realize we have seen a convincing portrait of a real human being."[64] Freedom for Thomas and Archy is not necessarily achieving safety from slavery but rather this life of constant pursuit, conflict, and danger. Theirs is not complete autonomy; it is the authority to retaliate with violence against a wealth of camouflaged enemies. While this world without limitations projects the lawlessness that Hildreth warns against throughout the novel, this image of a primitive world free of social constraints reflects an attraction to the land where the masculine ethos is the only governing principle.

Hildreth's treatment of men in the wilderness recalls Cooper's representation of the American landscape as the site of masculine encounter. But where Natty stands outside history, Archy is decidedly the product of history. The wilderness is merely one context in which Hildreth explores the nature of men and its implications for nation. Indeed, the novel's shift from violence in the context of society to violence in the wilderness offers a stark contrast that compels comparison between the institution of slavery, with its imbalance of power, and the wild, where men meet on the basis of equality. Hildreth is careful to distinguish the men's violent encounters in the wilderness from the tyranny of the slave regime. As Archy puts it, "[T]here is more of true manhood in the bold bosom of a single outlaw than in a whole nation of cowardly tyrants and crouching slaves!"[65] Through the depiction of Archy's life in the wilderness, Hildreth recontextualizes the desire for domination, undressing it and examining it outside of the context of social demands, only to demonstrate its incompatibility with social formations such as slavery. Hildreth's evocation of the frontier Eden juxtaposes an imaginary land of equality where men meet in the throes of mutual violence with the domination-subjugation scenario of slavery. In the wilderness, Archy and Thomas's violence is sanctioned by this equality, and thus is regenerative, while in the context of slavery, violence is degenerative. My interpretation of the regenerative quality of Archy's violence in the wilderness is influenced by Richard Slotkin, who argues that the myth of regeneration through violence becomes the "structuring metaphor of the American experience."[66] It is no coincidence that Hildreth depicts two slaves as regenerating their own sense of self and power in the world by means of violence; Hildreth evokes this image to force a comparison between the desires of early settlers and American slaves to make a call for emancipation. But Hildreth's characterization of the wilderness in comparison to his depiction of society suggests that violence beyond the homosocial world of the forest is degenerative as well. Hildreth's exclusion of women from this world points to the gender implications of this masculine landscape. It is as if social conventions are unnecessary in a world without the supposed inevitable imbalance of physical power that women would introduce. This depiction suggests that in a bigender world defined by masculine aggression, degeneration into a paradigm of domination versus submission is inevitable.

After his immersion in this lifestyle, Archy commits a final act that marks the development of his own version of aggressive manhood. He abandons Thomas, at Thomas's insistence, to travel north and pass as white. With the constant threat of being taken into slavery, Thomas recognizes that Archy's white skin would allow Archy a measure of safety that Thomas could not achieve on his own. While Archy reluctantly agrees and later regrets his decision to leave Thomas, his own desire to pursue freedom as a white man overwhelms him. Still, Archy's reluctance and disappointment in his abandonment of Thomas serves to embolden Archy's transition from slave to man. He does not abandon Thomas in selfish haste or cowardice; instead, it is only through Thomas's insistence that he is convinced to leave their life in the wilderness. Indeed, through Thomas's entreaties, Hildreth puts forth a sound argument for the advantages of passing that justifies Archy's actions. In the novel, passing as white is not portrayed as an act of weakness; instead, it is Archy's right and part of his newfound self-assertive manhood.

This manhood that Archy discovers in his apprenticeship with Thomas culminates in his murder of a ship captain who had once held him captive as a slave. Incredibly, Archy and his former foe reunite in battle, and upon discovering his opponent's identity, Archy relishes the act of penetrating the man with a sword mercilessly, though he has already subdued him. While this act of revenge serves as the final evidence of Archy's conversion from slave to man, Hildreth still straddles the line between the noble attributes of the release of such violent passions and their destructive potential. Reflecting on the act, Archy notes that "justice ought never to be sullied by passion,—and if possible, should be unstained with blood. If in my feelings at that moment there was something noble, there was far too much of savage fury and passionate revenge."[67] Hildreth celebrates Archy's thrilling victory, and yet he clearly finds it difficult to differentiate Archy's violence from the violent passions of Moore and others. While the ethical principle of such an act is measured by the towering image of the tyrannical slaveholder brutalizing the defenseless slave, the source of both acts in the context of the novel is unchecked and unpredictable "savage fury." It is difficult for Hildreth to reconcile the perpetuation of this ideology of masculinity and the concern for dangerous inner passions. But as the novel concludes, Archy is still in this cycle of pursuit, though perhaps from a more genteel vantage point. He has hired an agent to find Cassy, their son, and Thomas.

Though Hildreth's novel debuted to biting reviews and resistance to its extensive treatment of the sexual irregularities of slavery, this cliffhanger conclusion eventually led to a second volume that was appended to the first and entitled *Archy Moore, the White Slave; or, Memoirs of a Fugitive* (1856). With the success of *Uncle Tom's Cabin* (1852), one of the very publishers who had previously declined to publish the original novel suggested that Hildreth issue a sequel. By then the original had sold more than 7,000 copies and had been reprinted in the British periodical *The Truth Teller.* Its impact as the first full-length antislavery novel is undeniable. It sparked scores of works of antislavery fiction and mixed-race fiction. Hildreth's portrayal of mulatto figures as vehicles to explore the results of mysterious, uncontrolled desires that threaten the social structure illustrates how these characters massaged the American psyche, exploiting both fears and fantasies about the state of the nation.

3

Reconstructing America in Lydia Maria Child's *A Romance of the Republic* and Frances E. W. Harper's *Minnie's Sacrifice*

The quest to build a new nation during the Reconstruction era encouraged interest in a character that engaged the most pressing issue of the period, the role of race in the swiftly changing new union. Between 1865 and 1870, three amendments to the U.S. Constitution outlawed slavery, conferred civil rights to African Americans under the law, and granted suffrage to black men. Still, the question of what role blacks would play in this new nation was yet to be settled. Though the country saw dramatic changes, such as the election of sixteen blacks to Congress, the election of a black governor in Louisiana, and the establishment of black settlements, schools, and churches, many African Americans never obtained the right to vote and continued to labor for their former owners under exploitative conditions much like those they had experienced under slavery. In addition, violence by vigilante groups such as the Ku Klux Klan swept the South, demonstrating that white supremacist ideology still dominated the nation. Meanwhile, the controversy surrounding black men's suffrage had left a gaping rift in the women's movement. Racism fueled the activism of some women's rights leaders, such as Elizabeth Cady Stanton, who argued that white women were superior candidates for the right to vote.[1] The crisis of Reconstruction demonstrated that "the promised land was also the problematic land."[2]

It is not surprising that American writers engaged this turbulent era using mulatto figures, whose own shifting racial status mirrored the changing interpretations of race during this era. Mulatto characters that had previously been used to address the contradiction between slavery and American democracy were renewed and revised to consider the role of racial discrimination in the aftermath of the war. Lydia Maria Child's *A Romance of the Republic* (1867) and Frances E. W. Harper's *Minnie's Sacrifice* (1869) offer portraits of how each writer imagined the country's reconciliation. Through their treatment of mixed-race characters, these writers generate narratives of personal and national transition that parallel individual redefinitions of racial identity and the possibility of a national redefinition of the role of racial categories.

Child, a European-American writer, had been an active abolitionist, a women's rights activist, and a popular author of both adult and juvenile fiction. Her novel *A Romance of the Republic* is still considered by many to be the most radical of miscegenation texts because of its advocacy of interracial marriage. In the novel, she depicts mixed-race figures as symbols of the contradiction between the myth of America as a new Eden and the institution of slavery, but she also extends this premise to address American racial prejudice as evidence of the nation's failure to realize the dream of equality. Child focuses on the identity crises of mixed-race figures as they confront the categories of black and white, slave and free, calling attention to the crisis of identity that the nation faced during the Reconstruction era. But rather than dissolving, like her earlier mulatto heroines, when faced with slavery, these new mulattos survive; the means of survival is the acceptance and adaptability of both mixed-race figures and their white counterparts. Their endurance serves as a framework for the survival of the nation. Child's mulattos are not only figurative representations of a nation in transition, they also illustrate new Americans, ones who might celebrate hybridity rather than disintegrating in the face of categories that could not contain them. Child represents miscegenation as a fusing of bodily signs that would eventually nullify systems of racial categorization.

In contrast, Harper's novel rejects Child's representation of miscegenation as a framework for national reconciliation. Posing racial identity as cultural and psychological rather than bodily, Harper promotes the preservation of a unified African-American community that would prepare its members for the duties of national citizenship. Referencing the work of Child and others, whom she argues have endorsed the desertion of the black community by its more privileged, fair-skinned members, Harper signifies on these works, deeming them replications of "the old story."[3] Framing a new story for a new nation, Harper ironically looks to an old story, the biblical story of Moses, to model her novel.[4] By evoking this story, Harper called for cultural unity and political leadership that would demand the full civil participation of African Americans.

Mulattos in Eden

Both writers sought to revise mulatto characters in order to take into account the racial intolerance that riddled the postwar nation. Lydia Maria Child wrote of *A Romance of the Republic* that "[h]aving fought against slavery till I saw it go down in the Red Sea, I wanted to do something to undermine prejudice."[5] Though much of Child's text focuses on slavery, she envisioned her novel as an exploration of racial prejudice more than an exploration of slavery. Using the history of American slavery to remind readers of the horrific results of American racism, Child's novel asserts that to build a new nation, one that is not haunted by past sins, Americans would have to eradicate the lingering specter of racism.

As Carolyn Karcher notes, Child wrote the text in the midst of what many considered to be Andrew Johnson's betrayal of the Reconstruction effort and the nation's forgetfulness of its promises to blacks.[6] In resistance to Johnson's early retreat from Reconstruction policy, Child left a record of the horrors of slavery and of northern and southern involvement in the perpetuation of the institution. Juxtaposing the history of American slavery with her vision of an egalitarian state, Child reminds readers of the potential for America to fulfill its creed of liberty, and she admonishes her audience that it is possible to reenact the crimes of the past if racism is not conquered.

A Romance of the Republic revolves around two mulatto heroines, Rosa and Flora Royal, who initially have no knowledge of their black ancestry. The girls live with their father, Alfred Royal, who never informs them that their mother was a quadroon and his slave. As the story unfolds, the audience learns that as a young man, Royal was spurned by his white lover's family because he was not wealthy. He then purchased a quadroon mistress, Isabel, and the two settled in New Orleans. Rejected by polite society, the couple and their two daughters lived isolated in domestic bliss. After the death of both parents, the girls are to be sold at auction, but they are rescued by Gerald Fitzgerald, a young profligate. Fitzgerald and Rosa marry before their flight to the Georgia Sea Islands. Fitzgerald then arranges to buy Rosa and Flora from the creditors. When he has secured possession, he begins making advances toward Flora, threatening to sell her if she does not submit. Flora finds a guardian, who turns out to be her father's original white lover, the now-widowed Mrs. Delano. Whisked away to Europe, Flora escapes Fitzgerald, but Rosa is blissfully ignorant of Fitzgerald's intentions toward her sister until she discovers that Fitzgerald has taken a legal wife and that her own marriage to him was a sham. A pregnant Rosa escapes and becomes a celebrated opera singer in Europe and later marries a close family friend, Alfred King. Her child, who is initially left behind in the States, is lost later during a journey to join Rosa in Europe. Finally, Rosa and Flora return to the United States as happily married mothers and are reunited.

As Child's title indicates, she frames this account of mulatto figures as a story about the nation, centering on two paradisiacal settings that represent the notion of an American Eden. The New Orleans home of the girls is an extension of the garden that it overlooks, and the girls themselves become one with the burgeoning nature that surrounds them. They are called "human flowers," reinforcing their connection with the untainted natural world represented by their New Orleans home:

> The ample white lace curtains were surmounted by festoons of artificial roses, caught up by a bird of paradise. On the ceiling was an exquisitely painted garland from the centre of which hung a tasteful basket of natural flowers, with delicate vine-tresses drooping over its edge. The walls were papered with bright arabesque of flowers, interspersed with birds and butterflies. In one corner a statuette of Flora looked down upon a geranium covered with a profusion of rich blossoms. In the opposite corner, ivy was trained to form a dark background for Canova's "Dancer in Repose," over whose arm was thrown a wreath of interwoven vines and orange blossoms.[7]

Similar descriptions saturate Child's depiction of Flora and Rosa's Sea Island home, which is referred to as both the "Garden of Eden" and "paradise before the fall."[8]

Through this representation of mulattos in Eden, Child juxtaposes the myth of America as a new Eden with the limitations of American democracy. As Bruce Mills has pointed out, Child "preferred to change hearts primarily by inviting reflection upon the contradictions between the ideal and real narratives of American life."[9] By pointing to the social evils that underlie this supposed paradise, Child paints it as a false Eden, an illusion perpetuated by a well-intentioned father, but one who, as Andrea K. Newlyn has pointed out, fails to meet his paternal responsibilities.[10] Royal has not only deceived the girls into believing that they are free, he has also deluded himself into believing that he can protect them by keeping them cloistered in this environment. Since everyone knows of their heritage but the girls, Royal insists that they rarely go out, and when they do they must be heavily veiled to hide their identity. Their freedom is an illusion manufactured by Royal, and their seeming Eden is a well-disguised prison. Child exposes the fragility of this carefully constructed illusion when the girls are enslaved because their father fails to manumit them. By illustrating the girls' vulnerability, whether in the hands of a generous father or a malignant slaveholder, Child demonstrates how individual intentions are overwhelmed by the legislative power of the government; their legal designation as slaves consumes their domestic station as daughters.

Child's introduction of this Eden trope would have recalled her earlier 1842 work, "The Quadroons," a story that also revolves around two mixed-race heroines whose domestic paradise is destroyed by American politics, commerce, and law.[11] The short story tells of Rosalie, a young, beautiful, nearly white quadroon, who is courted by a white gentleman, Edward. They agree to a marriage that, because of their racial difference, is illegal in Georgia, where they live. The two settle in a quaint cottage surrounded by a rich tropical floral setting. Rosalie gives birth to a daughter, Xarifa, and all are happy until Edward suddenly becomes interested in politics and marries the daughter of an influential politician. Rosalie dies of grief, but the misfortune has only begun for Xarifa. Her father soon expires due to intemperance, leaving Xarifa unprotected. She is claimed as a slave by a family in debt. Apparently, her mother had never been legally freed. A tangled web of laws conspires to commit her to be the slave of a lustful tyrant who has sworn to make her his concubine. After her white lover, who is also her music teacher, is murdered while trying to rescue her, she takes her own life.

Like *A Romance of the Republic,* Child's short story couples the image of Eden with mulatto characters to illustrate numerous injustices that contradict American ideas of democracy and liberty. By juxtaposing a cultivated Eden with an inconstant outside world, Child exposes the chasm between myth and social reality. For Child, the world outside of Eden, the world of affairs, conspires to tempt and corrupt men, whose corruption is directly linked to the demise of the women who depend on them. The inability of Edward and other men to resist the temptations, such as politics, commerce, and slavery, which the American government endorses and depends upon, serves to pervert domestic bliss. At the root of this sense of corruption in the American government is the issue of race, the fulcrum on which the other disparate strands that contribute to Rosalie and Xarifa's tragic end pivot. Child provides a complicated cycle of events that stems from perceptions of race, mimicking the role of race in American culture. Because of antimiscegenation laws, Rosalie must trust the honor of Edward to ensure his fidelity and his obligation to her. Edward's interest in political life necessitates a legal marriage as well as a socially acceptable one, sparking his infidelity, which ruins not only the home of Rosalie but also that of his new bride. As the narrator foreshadows, Edward's pursuit of politics leads to his intemperance, leaving Xarifa exposed and claimed as a slave. This complicated chain of events illustrates how race as a tool of exclusion had become woven into an intricate system of laws and social life.

Though *A Romance of the Republic* also depends on this Eden trope to critique the American condition, the novel departs sharply from "The Quadroons." "The Quadroons" is part of Child's work that has led some critics to deem her the inventor of the "tragic mulatto," but in *A Romance of the Republic,* she converts a disastrous ending to an opportunity for a new beginning. Through such meaningful revisions, Child plots a new course for the nation. When this false Eden in *A Romance of the Republic* fails and reveals the corruption, prejudice, lust, and greed that lie beneath it, the mulatto figures do not dissolve; instead, they act in response to their new circumstances, and their white counterparts adjust as well.

Their self-preservation and desire to build new lives becomes a metaphor for Child's vision of what the union would have to do to survive the fall. Unlike Child's earlier heroines, who wither with the death of the false paradise, Rosa assesses her situation and responds to it. When Rosa discovers that she is Fitzgerald's slave rather than his wife, she begins to seek manumission for herself and for the protection of her unborn child. She not only refuses Gerald's pleas for her to accept the role of his quadroon mistress, she also defies his authority, risking being sold for her impudence. Rosa begins plans to effect her own escape, writing to friends under an assumed name for help. Though she contemplates suicide in a moment of despair upon discovering that Fitzgerald has sold her, she first thinks of murdering Fitzgerald. Instead, as a final act of revenge as she leaves him, she switches her child for Fitzgerald's white child, at once saving her own child and dooming Fitzgerald's to a life of slavery. While she regrets having done this, she makes no attempt to switch the children back. Finally, with the help of friends, she moves to Europe and earns her own living as a celebrated opera singer. Like Rosa, when Flora discovers that she is Fitzgerald's slave and thus subject to his will, she begins seeking methods of escape. Shocked and disgusted by Fitzgerald's attempts to initiate a sexual relationship with her, she creates shellwork to sell and earn money to finance her escape. Though the scheme is unsuccessful, it leads her to her benefactress, Mrs. Delano, who helps her escape.

Child's revisions are more than the insertion of happy endings for these mulatto figures. Casting Rosa's and Flora's survival as an allegory of national transition, Child's narrative maps scenarios of transition and renewal. The trope of identity transformation projects national Reconstruction. Rosa's and Flora's relationships to the whites who affect their happiness provide examples of the duties of white Americans in the postwar era. Though Rosa and Flora do not wither with the revelation of their bondage, they depend upon Mrs. Delano and Alfred King for their safety. While Rosa makes her own way to Europe and supports herself as an opera singer, it is Alfred King whose wealth allows her to leave the stage and become a genteel wife. It is significant that Child poses both King and Delano as having been initially ambivalent about slavery and racism and deeply concerned about social codes of propriety. Though King immediately falls in love with Rosa upon meeting her as a young man, when he discovers soon after that she is mixed, he cannot imagine breaking with social propriety to pursue her. Similarly, Mrs. Delano is reluctant to join the abolitionist cause until she meets Flora and discovers that she is a slave. Both Delano and King have to overcome their racial prejudice to make new beginnings with these women, and both are rewarded with domestic happiness.

Dark Passion

While Child presents mulatto figures as metaphors for a nation in transition, she also depicts them as the merger of supposed racial traits. The novel's focus on shifting racial identities is not as much about race as an idea or an interpretation as it is about how miscegenated bodies may combine the talents, tastes, and demeanor that are supposedly essential to each racial group. Like most of her contemporaries, Child represents race as real. It is a series of elements transmitted genetically and thus capable of being reproductively manipulated. It is through this process that a new American might be born or perhaps negotiated in Child's novel.

Child depicts race as a determinant of human behaviors by presenting traits that become racialized throughout the book. Even the novel's Eden becomes the site of racial essentialism, associating the voluptuous natural scenes and unrestrained sensual experiences with people of African descent. While white characters join in these scenes, they do so as observers. It is the mulatto figures who become one with the sensuality of nature. The novel's opening scene in which their father and his guests Fitzgerald and King are entertained by the girls exemplifies how the girls melt into the scenery around them:

> Rosabella's white muslin dress was trailed all over with delicately tinted roses and the lace around the corsage was fastened in front with a mosaic basket of flowers. Floracita's black curls fell over her shoulders mixed with crimson fuchsias, and on each of her little slippers was embroidered a bouquet.[12]

Repeatedly the girls are referred to as "tropical flowers," and the girls' names, Rosa and Flora, confirm this analogy.[13] The connotations of the allusion are also manifested in the passion and sensuality of their characters. Flora dances impulsively, "as if the music had made [her dance] without her choice," providing "such exquisite pleasure, that all had been absorbed in watching," and Rosa plays the piano and sings with "so much feeling" that all listeners are in awe of her.[14] Such representations imply the girls' latent sexuality. Passionate, colorful, impulsive, and sensual, Rosa and Flora, like the gardens they live in, are in need of taming. Child's effort to temper that portrayal by referring to the girls' overt innocence suggests her recognition of the connotations of this depiction. Even though they are innocent, their passionate spirits insinuate a flourishing sexuality that is mitigated only partially by their naiveté.

Child's portrayal of Rosa and Flora as performers compounds their objectification. Not only are they surrounded by sensual imagery, they also provide sensual pleasure for the men. Their performances are not limited to their youthful years or to audiences of men. In fact, they and their daughters perform in both public and private settings. The depiction of Rosa and Flora as performers for whites recalls minstrelsy, or black confinement to performance roles in the lives of whites. And as female performers, Rosa and Flora become sexualized in a way that distinguishes them from the white women characters; they become objects that exist for the sensual pleasure of others. As Karcher has noted, the portrayal of Rosa as an opera singer makes her little better than a prostitute.[15] On display for the entertainment and scrutiny of whites, Rosa trades the auction block for the opera stage.

Because Child racializes Rosa's singing talent with the suggestion that it is the legacy of her black heritage, the portrayal becomes doubly indicative of the limitations of the racial prescription imposed upon these characters. When Gerald Fitzgerald arrives at his plantation with his new wife and Rosa begins singing in utter anguish over his deceit, Gerald responds to his wife's inquiries about who the singer is with "One of the darkies I suppose. . . . You know they all have musical gifts."[16] When his wife is not satisfied, he adds, "They are nearly all musical, and wonderfully imitative."[17] While Gerald's role as the villain in the novel suggests that he is not a credible interpreter of the novel's representation of the girls, the narrative reference to Rosa's biracial protégé, Hen, echoes his statement: "and belonging to an imitative race, [Hen] readily adopted the language and manners of those around her."[18] Even their father takes pride in Rosa's and Flora's talent for imitation, calling Rosa "a musical ventriloquist."[19] The qualities Rosa and Flora and "the darkies" share remind readers that for Child, as for many others, racial equality meant disregarding innate difference rather than the eradication of racial essentialism.

The consistency in the portrayal of Rosa and Flora and their daughters as performers throughout the novel coupled with the absence of any white girls or women who repeatedly serve to pleasure others suggest that blackness becomes the validation for Rosa's and Flora's position as entertainers for whites. While Dana Nelson asserts that Rosa's and Flora's constant performances of song and dance recall the role of women in marriage and allow Child to critique male privilege, Rosa's and Flora's performances for white women imply that white privilege rather than masculine privilege entitles one to gaze upon their bodies.[20] The white women in the novel serve as foils for Rosa's and Flora's dark beauty, rich colored clothing, and sensual natures. Mrs. Delano, Flora's reserved guardian, is the model of New England propriety, and her pale beauty, conservative dress, and passionless manner suggest an undergirding theory of biological difference. Similarly, the pale blonde Lily, Fitzgerald's legitimate bride, functions as Rosa's antithesis. Portrayed as having a voice that did not compare to the rich tones of Rosa's, Lily is characterized as a socialite so absorbed with polite society that she is incapable of any real depth of feeling other than jealousy and possessiveness, in contrast to Rosa's passionate spirit. The passionlessness of these white women only serves to enhance the peculiarity of Rosa's and Flora's sensuality and ardor. Child repeatedly suggests that biological difference, rather than cultural disparity, is what shapes the lives of Flora, Rosa, and their daughters. When Flora says to Mrs. Delano that she could have been her mother, Mrs. Delano replies: "You call me the Java sparrow, and Java sparrows never hatch gay little humming-birds or tuneful mocking-birds," suggesting a profound innate difference between them.[21] Although Flora to some degree changes Mrs. Delano's ambivalent feelings about slavery, Mrs. Delano cannot change Flora. After trying to give Flora a proper New England education, Mrs. Delano says, "It is a hopeless undertaking to educate her after the New England pattern. One might as well try to plough with a butterfly as to teach her ancient history."[22] Flora is not suited to intellectual development, and all of Mrs. Delano's powers cannot change her. Despite her annoyance at Flora's uninhibited behavior, Mrs. Delano resolves to stop checking her because it would "spoil the naturalness which makes her so charming."[23]

According to Karcher, Child's portrayal of Flora as incapable of conforming to social standards of ladylike behavior projects Child's own desire for unfettered being. Karcher notes that Child struggled with her own "dammed up" sexuality, creating utopian worlds in which sexual desires could enjoy free play in order to address her feelings of sexual repression.[24] While Rosa and Flora do not necessarily enjoy complete sexual freedom, certainly the evidence of their sexuality and the natural paradise surrounding them illustrates optimistic possibilities in comparison to Child's world. It is significant that the objects of Child's fantasies of female sexual liberty are characters of African descent who come to represent the antithesis of Anglo-American repression exhibited in Child's white characters.

From Slave Trade to Gene Trade

There is nothing really unusual about this representation of racial signs or distinct qualities that nearly white bodies fail to conceal, but what is intriguing is that Child presents them as a sort of smorgasbord of racial possibilities. They are signs that point the way not to inevitable racial condemnation but rather to the possibility of biological mediation. Child's exploration of miscegenation promotes the notion of a gene trade, or an exchange of hereditary traits, as a plan for a reconstructed America. Here, I borrow Octavia Butler's concept of "the trade" in her Xenogenesis trilogy, in which both human and alien survival depends on cross-species reproduction.[25] The term is particularly relevant here because of its emphasis on exchange and its result, a new being who is better suited to the bicultural world and perhaps is the beginning of the end of a biracial/bicultural world. Child represents cross-racial hereditary intersections as a trade of both physiognomy and character traits that will eventually reduce bodily evidence of race into a series of signless parts, liquefying and reformulating the signs of identity. Ultimately, her mulatto figures represent the transmission of bodily signs that throw the system of racial categorization into flux. In Child's ideal world this genetic exchange will produce a more harmonious nation that is no longer divided by racial distinctions.

Child's vision of interracialism as a means to racelessness is problematic. Indeed, Child's version of this emerging racelessness looks an awful lot like phenotypic whiteness. At the novel's conclusion, Rosa and Flora live as white and assume a "don't ask, don't tell" policy regarding racial background; they do not even tell their children anything of their past. The gene trade becomes another form of the slave trade, as the white characters, such as Flora's guardian, Mrs. Delano, shop for the characteristics that they believe would improve the merchandise—not by training, but by breeding. Mrs. Delano chooses a man of German descent to be Flora's husband. She finances his career, establishing him as a prosperous businessman and an appropriate mate for Flora. Thus, Mrs. Delano also produces the fair-skinned progeny of this union, the children who she claims as her grandchildren. Throughout the novel, there are detailed descriptions of each child of a mixed-race union. The descriptions suggest subtle combinations of traits associated with African and European ancestry. Speaking with her husband about her daughter, Flora points out her "German blue eyes, and the fine frizzle of curly light hair." She remarks, "Your great-grandmother gave her the flax, and I suppose mine did the frizzling."[26] It is significant that the few men of African descent in the novel, including Rosa's son, who dies in the war, are completely eliminated from this scheme. Only female mulatto bodies are colonized to produce paler and paler offspring.

Mixing a Nation

The marriages of both Rosa and Flora propose miscegenation as a solution to the national situation. Carolyn Karcher notes that the scheme fails because Child understood that marriage was an inequitable institution. I argue, however, that for this very reason, marriage does serve as a model for the paternalistic arrangement that Child imagines between whites and African Americans. Child's portrait of America is not a marriage of equals but a condescending relationship in which one party is forever responsible for the other. Though both King and Delano find happiness only when they overcome their prejudices, the paternalism of their treatment of Rosa and Flora is pervasive. And more disturbing, the means of their control over these women is financial. Mrs. Delano manages Flora's life, even financing a partnership in a local business firm for one of her admirers so that he would become an adequate husband. As Karcher has pointed out, King's paternalism is excessive.[27] Ultimately King replaces the failed father figure, taking up the paternal responsibilities that Rosa's father neglected. Child portrays their relationship as a familial connection, void of sexual passion, highlighting the importance of his paternal duty over a lover's enthusiasm.

The schema of gene trade/slave trade marriage extends to Child's final attempt to represent the road to racial equality, a daring portrayal of an interracial marriage between a white man and a brown-skinned mulatto woman. When Rosa confesses to having switched the children, her husband sets out to correct the wrong by finding the white child that Rosa had exchanged with her own and repaying the inheritance due him as the rightful heir of the Fitzgerald estate. The heir who had been sold into slavery, George Falkner, is found, and the King family decides to train him and his dark-skinned mixed-race wife to enter society in Europe. To make reparations for Rosa's crime, her husband Alfred King vows to educate George and his wife Hen, set George up as partner in his business, and send them both to Europe, where they can live free of American color prejudice. While George serves in the Union army, the Kings begin training Hen, whom they always respectfully refer to as Mrs. Falkner, to play the piano and generally to be what Tulee, a servant of the Kings, calls "'spectable out there 'mong strangers."[28] Belonging to an "imitative race," Hen quickly learns to speak as the Kings do and to write neatly.[29]

As Karcher points out, the Kings' benevolence toward the Falkners smacks of paternalism, especially as King proceeds to dictate a lengthy list of rules to George before he goes to Europe, even rationing George's rightful inheritance because he, Mrs. Delano, and Flora's husband, Florimond Blumenthal, conclude that the Falkners will squander their money.[30] The Falkners are never consulted about their own future, and the Kings withhold knowledge of the Falkners' inheritance and the details of George's ancestry from them. In addition, Hen's progress is repeatedly put on display for the scrutiny of the whites, especially the white men.[31]

Even more disturbing about this episode is the differentiation made between Hen and the black servants of the Kings, Tulee, Chloe, and Tom. When Chloe sees Hen learning to play the piano, she is jealous because her own children were not afforded the same privilege and remarks: "I didn't know Missy Rosy tought thar war sech a mighty difference 'tween black an' brown . . . I don't see nothin so drefful pooty in dat ar molasses color."[32] Though Tulee withholds crucial information, to some degree her story is true. The Kings see themselves as repaying George not just for his friendship with Gerald during the war but for the inheritance that Rosa stole from him and bestowed on her own child. They feel no need to repay Tulee or Chloe beyond making them legally free, though the two had nursed Rosa from near-death. Although they are supposedly free, Tulee, Chloe, and Tom still work as domestic servants in the same household as they did when they were slaves. While their children go to school, they too are described as household servants. Rosa considers their employment as servants to be their reward for their kind service to her, thanking her husband for hiring them: "O Alfred . . . I am so grateful to you for employing them all! You don't know, and never *can* know, how I feel toward these dusky friends; for you never had them watch over you, day after day."[33]

Child's portrayal of Hen seems more concerned with reinstating white privilege by returning George's stolen inheritance than it is concerned with racial reform. Considering that King repeatedly states that if the money could be returned, the affair could be "managed as to do no very serious harm," thus denying the horror of George's enslavement, it is not surprising that they make no effort to repay the other former slaves for their bondage.[34] Hen has the fortune of being married to a white man who has been misplaced. Though their loving marriage and the kindness that the Kings show to the Falkners offers a vision of intraracial unity, a white man's inheritance takes precedence over what the blacks have been robbed of through enslavement, and their acts of benevolence reestablish a hierarchy in which monetary power is valued over human emotional lives, the very structure that fueled slavery.

While Child's portrayal of Hen's successful imitation of white middle-class values aims to demonstrate the potential for blacks to advance with education during the Reconstruction, Hen is presented as a vacuous figure with no values of her own and desperately in need of white guidance. Though several of Child's characters mention how contact between the races will also cause "improvement in the white population," we see little change brought about by the nonwhite characters.[35] Mrs. Delano's feelings about slavery change, but it is only because Flora at first sight appears to be white and is also a victim of slavery. Unlike Flora, Hen is neither white nor beautiful, and her only value is in her ability to imitate whites and annihilate any trace of black culture. Although Flora cannot be tamed, it seems that whiteness and beauty excuse her, while evidence of Hen's cultural blackness is intolerable.

The child of George and Hen also detracts from Child's vision of racial equality by further affirming the whitening of America that she envisions. Their daughter, little Hetty, is described as a "pretty little creature" with "black curls" that "shook" and "coral lips."[36] In contrast, Hen is described thus: "Her features were not handsome, with the exception of her dark, liquid-looking eyes; and her black hair was too crisp to make a soft shading for her brown forehead."[37] Though Hen's skin is yellow, she is certainly a part of this trajectory toward whiteness, the goal of racial mixing in Child's text. The difference between Hen and the other blacks is that as the wife of a white man, she has the potential to legitimately have a visibly white descendant and therefore she should be afforded the privileges that she can bestow upon them.

Hen reverts to the status of the property and responsibility of the white characters in the novel, while her white husband returns to his rightful role as white heir and descendant of slaveowners. The marriage of Hen and George Falkner encapsulates both the novel's enthusiastic belief in the potential for America to become an egalitarian nation and its failure to imagine a social system that did not mimic the master/slave roles of slavery.

A Romance of the Republic is both a sign of the eager desire to build a new nation that could escape its dark past of racial violence and damning evidence of what a long journey that would be.

"The Old Story"

Just two years after *A Romance of the Republic* appeared in 1867, Frances E. W. Harper, who was at the time America's most popular black writer, serialized *Minnie's Sacrifice* (1869). Harper, born to free parents in Baltimore, Maryland, in 1825, was a poet, essayist, novelist, short-story writer, and orator. She was also an activist for causes such as antislavery, women's rights, temperance, and civil rights. Like her later and most well-known novel, *Iola Leroy, Minnie's Sacrifice* exhibits a distinct intersection between Harper's activism and her fiction. Concerned with the transition from slavery to freedom, *Minnie's Sacrifice* focuses on mixed-race characters to posit a model for the nation's quest for a new identity and to illustrate African-American cultural unity and advancement. Harper's representation of mixed-race characters expresses a vision of nation that includes both a rehabilitated America ready to extend the rights of citizenship to all of its citizens and an improved African-American community prepared to participate fully in an egalitarian state.

Minnie's Sacrifice tells the story of a mixed-race man and woman who, unaware of their racial heritage, live their lives as white until they discover their African ancestry and dedicate themselves to racial uplift. Two plots intertwine in the novel: Louis, the child of a union between the recently deceased Agnes and her master, is adopted by the master, the wealthy slaveowner LeCroix, at the insistence of his daughter Camilla, who is unaware that Louis is her half-brother. Louis, who has never been told that he has African ancestry, travels as a young man in the North, where he meets Minnie, the adopted daughter of a Quaker family. In the second plot, Minnie, also the child of a beautiful quadroon slave and her owner, is sent to the North by her father when she is very young. Without any memory of her first years of life spent on the plantation, she is unaware of her African lineage. After Minnie and Louis discover their African ancestry, they marry and go to the South to help newly freed blacks during Reconstruction. But their joyful initiation as black community leaders is interrupted when Minnie is killed by a racist vigilante group.[38] Though grief-stricken, Louis continues his commitment to the development of the rural black community where he lives.

From its beginning, *Minnie's Sacrifice* initiates intertextual dialogue with other writers of mulatto fiction. Opening with a familiar, though condensed version of a mulatto fiction plot, Harper's novel begins:

> It was the old story. Agnes fair, young, and beautiful had been a slave with no power to protect herself from the highest insults that brutality could offer to innocence. Bound hand and foot by that system, which has since gone down in wrath, and blood, and tears, she had fallen a victim to the wiles and power of her master; and the result was the introduction of a child of shame into a world of sin and suffering; for herself an early grave; and for her mother a desolate breaking heart.[39]

Harper's use of the term "the old story" harkens back not only to slavery but also to the popular stories of mixed-race heroines who were seduced or raped by unscrupulous men. Her acknowledgment of previous mulatto fiction at the outset of her novel deliberately places *Minnie's Sacrifice* in conversation with such works. By reducing a plot that had filled 500-page novels to a single paragraph, Harper calls attention to her own deliberate revision of such fiction. Harper's desire to situate her own story of national reconstruction and reconciliation in relation to other mulatto fiction demonstrates her recognition of the ways in which mulatto fiction engaged the national implications of race. Thus, Harper suggests her participation in and transmutation of that convention. While some critics have considered the use of mulatto characters as a concession to white audiences, Harper's conscious evocation of previous mulatto fiction indicates the ways in which mulatto fiction allowed writers to enter into conversation with other writers and with their audiences about the significance of race in America. The epilogue of *Minnie's Sacrifice* confirms this intention of intertextual communication:

> While some of the authors of the present day have been weaving their stories about white men marrying beautiful quadroon girls, who, in so doing

> were lost to us socially, I conceived of one of that same class to whom I gave a higher, holier destiny; a life of lofty self-sacrifice and self-consecration, finished at the post of duty and rounded off with the fiery crown of martyrdom, a circlet which ever changes into a diadem of glory.[40]

In conjunction with Harper's reference to the "old story," her use of the term "the present day" questions the relevance of the "old story" to "the present day," or the relevance of the abolitionist story to the Reconstruction era. Harper's criticism of interracial fictions such as Child's points to Harper's aim to renovate those stories to challenge their implications for the nation.

With the phrase "lost to us," Harper calls attention to her most distinct revision, her inclusion of the black community, which is absent in much mulatto fiction. In "The Quadroons," for example, absolutely no people are identified as black, and though Child's later work *A Romance of the Republic* includes black characters, the audience sees only brief glimpses of a black community because mixed-race and white characters remain in the foreground and black characters are largely viewed in relation to them. This invisibility of the black community suggests the silencing and objectification of black people. Even in William Wells Brown's *Clotel,* in which there are black characters and a black plantation community, the antagonism between the darker characters and the mixed-race ones as well as the white lovers that Althesa and Clotel take serves to establish a distinct rift between the black and mulatto characters. Harper's portrayal of mulatto figures as part of a larger black community as in her later work *Iola Leroy* is a distinct departure from these works.

In place of "the old story," Harper affixes a plot that is even older by initiating an account that recalls the story of Moses. When Camilla decides to rescue Louis from slavery, she refers to the rescue of Moses, saying "I mean to do something like that good princess."[41] Like Moses, both Minnie and Louis, who have the advantages of being adopted members of the dominant social group, dedicate their lives to the future of the oppressed group from which they descended.[42] Harper's use of the story of Moses, which had become both a proponent of cultural unity and a call for internal leadership among blacks, illuminates her concern with the place of black communities within the larger nation. Reconstruction had reentrenched blacks' adoption of the biblical story of the Israelites because its emphasis on community leadership harmonized with the need for black political agency.[43] But while Harper highlights the improvement of the black community, her emphasis on their equal participation in U.S. political life through the guidance of black leaders reflects a duality that characterized many blacks' vision of themselves and their ideal place in the United States during the Reconstruction era. Because many blacks preserved a sense of distinct racial identity while also imagining a political system purged of racial distinctions, the Moses narrative's emphasis on the need for community leadership also signifies the quest for equal participation under the law.[44] Harper's use of the narrative not only posits a call for race leaders and a unified black political agenda, it also offers a vision of a path to an inclusive American democratic process.

By combining the Moses paradigm with mulatto characters, Harper suggests the integral relationship between whites and blacks to argue for an egalitarian nation. Just as Moses is of two worlds, Egyptian and Israelite, Louis and Minnie bear relation to both blacks and whites. As mulatto figures, Louis and Minnie convey both the double consciousness of African-American experience and the reality of a multiracial nation. By making Louis and Camilla biological siblings as well as adopted ones, Harper conveys both the bonds between white and black Americans and the potential for reconciliation and equality between the two groups. This sentiment reflects Harper's feelings, which she articulated while lecturing in the South during the Reconstruction era: "I hold that between the white people and the colored there is a community of interests, and the sooner they find it out, the better it will be for both parties."[45] Harper's intersection of the Moses figure and mulatto characters offers a unified community that exists within the boundaries of another.

The Moses story also bridges the domestic and political worlds by rejecting the paradigm of separate worlds that emerges in other mulatto fiction based on the Eden paradigm. The trope of the invasion of the domestic space by the world of affairs is nullified by Harper's use of a story that combines domestic and public space through the union of a woman's adoption of a child and that child's destined future as a political leader. The coherence of these spaces suggests a more gender-inclusive vision of American life.

This sense of the relationship between personal lives and political change characterizes Harper's portrayal of Minnie and Louis, whose identity transformation mirrors the Civil War. In *Minnie's Sacrifice,* each of the central characters must undergo a transformation that frequently resembles the drastic and violent transformation that the country has undergone, and each character must build a new life that stems from their new vision of themselves and their place in the world in relation to others, just as the country must convert the war into a new beginning. Offering the personal biographies of her characters as archetypes for a new post-Reconstruction nation, Harper poses Minnie and Louis as microcosmic examples of the country's journey toward a new identity. In reference to her discovery of her racial heritage, Minnie calls this sorrowful period one of the most fruitful in her life saying, "Oh, there are lessons of life that we never learn in the bowers of ease. They must be learned in the fire. . . . [I]n those days of pain and sorrow my resolution was formed to join the fortunes of my mother's race."[46] The focus here is not Minnie's victimization but on her rebirth in a baptism of fire, an image which Harper later uses to describe the Civil War.

This pairing of examples of personal renewal with the state of the nation is indicative of Harper's contention that national change would come through individual growth.[47] The theme of transition and rebirth allows Harper to use individual fictive lives to chart a course for a nation at a critical juncture. Just as Minnie and Louis must decide whether they will deny and hide their racial ancestry or accept and acknowledge it, the nation must decide whether it will continue to self-identify as a white nation or accept the reality of a multiracial one.

Minnie bears a striking contrast to many mulatto heroines. While not all mulatto fiction includes the racial discovery plot, when it is included in texts such as John Trowbridge's *Neighbor Jackwood* (1857), H. L. Hosmer's *Adela the Octoroon* (1860), Child's *A Romance of the Republic* (1867), and even Harper's own later novel *Iola Leroy* (1892), the discovery often leads to the heroine's confrontation with the threat of slavery and sexual abuse. In contrast, Minnie, unlike her mother, is not exposed to the tyranny of a white man, and her virtue is never challenged by slavery. Though she suffers after the discovery of her racial ancestry, Minnie's struggle is largely internal. Furthermore, the transition is assuaged by Minnie's reunion with her loving mother, who unintentionally reveals Minnie's racial background. Rather than the separation and isolation from loved ones that many mixed-race figures experience, Minnie gains a new mother in addition to her adopted one. Minnie's heroism is not a response to abuse but is rather the call of duty to African Americans. By focusing on Minnie's struggle with issues of duty and self-sacrifice, Harper shifts the emphasis from sexual violation to interior ethical issues that highlight the need for national reconciliation and renewal.

Harper poses Minnie's commitment, her personal and public sacrifice, as an example of what is incumbent upon all Americans, who must commit themselves to building a nation. Minnie is transformed from white to black, from an apologetic observer of the black condition to an active participant in rebuilding the black community and nation. Having lived as both a black woman and a white woman, Minnie's claim to leadership serves as a model to all because her life represents the unifying experience of the war that all Americans had suffered through. Harper creates a multiracial model of women's agency, arguing for the potential productivity of a unified resistance to racial and gender oppression. The joint relationship between the civil rights of women and blacks in America is a poignant theme in the novel. In a discussion of Reconstruction politics, Minnie argues that while the country is building itself anew, it should revise the current civil status of women as well as African Americans. When Louis retorts, "This hour belongs to the negro," Minnie reminds him that blacks and women are not mutually exclusive groups, saying, "is it not the negro woman's hour also? Has she not as many rights and claims as the negro man?"[48] Minnie defies the notion of the passive female mulatto figure, just as Brown's Clotel does. But unlike Clotel, Minnie is not plotting to escape slavery, disguising herself as a man, or seeking to free her daughter. Instead, Minnie is arguing with her loving husband for women's suffrage. Harper redefines female resistance here to include more than responses to physical bondage; her version of resistance includes the struggle for equal political rights for women.

Still, as do the earlier plots that Harper evokes in her opening, Minnie dies an untimely death, leaving behind a grieving husband and community. Harper frames her death, however, as a Christ-like sacrifice in the name of an oppressed people and for the betterment of the nation. By representing Minnie's death as a sacrifice to a larger cause rather than an individual response to sexual degradation, Harper remolds the sense of catastrophe that is associated with works such as Child's "The Quadroons"; while personal affliction implicates the problems of the state in "The Quadroons," Harper equates personal affliction with national loss. Because the text suggests that Minnie is killed by a southern vigilante group such as the Ku Klux Klan, Minnie's death also portrays the undeniable violence that plagued the nation. For Harper, Minnie must be sacrificed to demonstrate the reality that though this nation "passed through the fire," its "troubles are not over yet."[49]

Minnie's role as savior of her people also distinguishes her from mulatto heroines who are defined by their sexuality. While Nancy Bentley argues that "tragic mulattas" achieve spiritual transcendence through the sexual violation of their bodies, I would submit that the taint of sexual degradation is not always entirely effaced from mulatto characters through death.[50] In fact, in Child's "The Quadroons," the burial of Rosalie is described thus: "She had often expressed to her daughter a wish to be buried under a spreading oak, that shaded a rustic garden-chair in which she and Edward had spent many happy evenings. And there she was buried; with a small white cross at her head, twined with the cypress vine."[51] Rosalie's sexuality is maintained as her definitive characteristic in this passage; flora is the central symbol of her sexuality in the short story, and she is buried near the site where her love affair began. Sexual degradation does not lead to the death and spiritual transcendence of Stowe's Cassy of *Uncle Tom's Cabin* (1852): instead she achieves spiritual renewal through motherhood. Clotel's male pursuers begin to celebrate her capture and fantasize about her punishment even before she is caught, highlighting the constant sexual threat that faced her from the moment she was sold into slavery. For many of these characters, the possibility of transcendence is capped by the lingering image of sexual vulnerability and perhaps culpability.

In contrast, the implied absence of sexual pursuit in conjunction with the emphasis on her contribution to the community suggests that despite the circumstances of her death, Minnie achieves transcendence without the taint of sexual violation and that her spiritual transcendence precedes her death. Minnie has already sacrificed her life to the progress of her community before her death. Her death is only a symbol of the sacrifice she has already made and a marker of southern violence. The final chapter as well as Harper's conclusion confirm the emphasis on Minnie's gift to the community by foregrounding those who she had helped:

> Surely, thought Louis, if the blessings and tears of the poor and needy and the prayers of him who was ready to perish would crystallize a path to the glory-land, then Minnie's exit from earth must have been over a bridge of light, above whose radiant arches hovering angels would delight to bend.[52]

National Reconciliation

Like Minnie, Louis shares this commitment to the uplift of blacks, but initially his southern sentiments about slavery and the rights of the confederacy bias him. Before discovering his African heritage, Louis had decided to join the Confederate army. Just as Minnie eventually espouses her devotion to blacks because she sees them as the same race as her mother, Louis calls the South his mother, saying, "[T]hat man is an ingrate who will not stand by his mother and defend her when she is in peril."[53] When Louis finds out that his mother was a black slave, he withdraws from the Confederate cause, and yet he feels no sympathy with the North or with blacks, whom he imagines as his inferiors. As he escapes north as a Confederate deserter with the help of black strangers who are faithful to the northern cause, he is overwhelmed by their loyalty and bravery and begins to reconsider his views on racial difference.

By depicting Louis as a Confederate sympathizer who gradually accepts racial equality, Harper suggests the possibility that former Confederates could grow with the progress of the new nation. In addition, by framing Louis's allegiance as his loyalty to his mother country rather than as his faith in the slave system, Harper represents his love for the confederacy as misguided rather than malicious. Mitigating the importance of former allegiances, Harper foregrounds reconciliation in the novel. After the war, upon returning to the plantation where he grew up, Louis introduces Minnie to the slave who was formerly known to him as Aunt Miriam as his grandmother. Louis's recognition of his relationship to Miriam as a blood relation rather than as a servant and a slave mirrors Harper's vision for the new nation, one in which old relationships of master and slave could be reenvisioned in terms of equality. By transforming Miriam from mammy figure to mother figure, Harper highlights the intimate ties between former slaveowners and their slaves as a foundation for racial equality. Louis's feeling that "that man is an ingrate who will not stand by his mother and defend her when she is in peril" can be read as an admonition to former slaveholders who were raised and nurtured by black caretakers.[54]

As Louis escapes north after his desertion of the Confederate Army, Harper expands the figurative possibilities of his racial ambiguity, posing him as a heroic slave figure escaping to the North.[55] Though Louis initially scorns his black heritage and considers blacks his inferiors, on his journey north, blacks become his saviors, risking their lives when he tells them that he is black. As Louis progresses from paternalism to beneficence, his admiration for their faithfulness and bravery inspires him to identify himself as black and commit to the cause of black civil rights. As in slave narratives, Louis's journey north symbolizes his rebirth, but in this case he is reborn as a black man. The multiple interpretations of Louis's personal transition, from confederate to black sympathizer and from free white man to black slave and then to free black man, suggest Harper's intention to use Louis's story to encompass the journeys of many Americans as the nation passed through the war.

Though Harper's mulatto characters become useful tools in addressing the nation's treatment of race, her characterization of them also fosters a class hierarchy that she would still be struggling with in her 1892 novel *Iola Leroy.* Considering that Minnie and Louis have only recently discovered their heritage and decided to live as black, their authority as black leaders seems questionable. Rather than simply joining a community of black workers, Minnie and Louis immediately assume the role of leaders in a community that they know nothing about. While Louis becomes a political organizer, Minnie assumes the role of model homemaker for the women. Neither have any formal training in these fields, and Minnie has no children of her own, though she professes to be able to teach former slave women who have not only been caretakers for their own children but also for white children for generations. Louis's role as a political leader is puzzling, considering how little time has passed since he avowed that blacks were better off as slaves because they could not govern themselves. Clearly, Minnie and Louis's white middle-class upbringing is the source of their authority over these former slaves, who passively accept their leadership. The color hierarchy that stems from this portrayal is also disturbing. Kimberly A. C. Wilson has asserted that the similar characterization of the mulatto figures in *Iola Leroy* demonstrates Harper's capitulation to the "assumption that a white readership has greater worth than any other audience."[56] The publication of *Minnie's Sacrifice,* however, in *The Christian Recorder,* an African-American newspaper, challenges this assumption. Despite the fluidity of race displayed through Harper's characters, the markers of class stay firmly intact, and, unfortunately, the codes of color frequently follow suit. Harper outlines one subject about which Minnie realizes she must be taught by the former slaves: spirituality. Yet even in matters of faith, it is Minnie who becomes the savior of freed people through her death rather than vice versa. Even in the spiritual realm Minnie remains their superior. Just as Child's text cannot escape prevalent racial ideologies, Harper's novel bears marks of class hierarchy.

A Romance of the Republic and *Minnie's Sacrifice* illuminate the ways in which the representation of mixed-race characters allowed writers to engage in conversations about the impact of racial categories on the national character. As signs of transition, mulatto figures not only captured the national crisis of identity, they also functioned as figurative representations of the interracial unity that these writers hoped would be born from the fire of the Civil War. The use of mulatto figures allowed these writers multiple ways of exploring the significance of racial difference by participating in and revising a literary tradition. In *A Romance of the Republic,* Child transforms the devastation of slavery into a story of reunion and reconciliation between the races. Harper manipulates the conventions of mulatto fiction to address issues that faced black communities as they sought to negotiate their place within the larger nation. But while Child's novel focuses on the possibility of radical social transformations fueled by the interracial marriages of paternalistic whites and grateful blacks, Harper's works promote the potential agency of unified black communities in the struggle for civil rights. By regenerating the stories of mulatto fiction, Child and Harper created new stories that spoke to the Reconstruction era and challenged popular perceptions of race and difference. In *Minnie's Sacrifice,* the story of Moses inspires Camilla to spare Louis from a life of slavery and envision herself as a liberator. By revising "the old story," these writers designed their stories to have this kind of rhetorical power to force readers, black and white, to reimagine themselves and to commit to the cause of liberation.

4

Doubles in Eden in George Washington Cable's *The Grandissimes*

After the Reconstruction era ended and political control returned to the South in 1877, writers of mulatto fiction confronted a nation seeking new ways to redefine the social order. Law and custom continued to inform and be informed by the myth of race. Laws were enacted to ensure racial segregation and prohibit the civil rights of blacks. In addition, lynching terrorized African Americans, demonstrating the growing rage that fueled attempts to maintain the color line. It is no surprise that this period produced a wealth of mulatto fiction by writers that included William Dean Howells, Mark Twain, Charles Chesnutt, Kate Chopin, and Pauline Hopkins. Southern writer George Washington Cable was no exception. In *The Grandissimes* (1879), Cable frames a concern with the relationship between race and the national condition by evoking the image of mulattos in Eden. Pairing these mulatto figures with their white half-siblings, Cable explores the color line in the increasingly segregated society of his time. In each relationship, the white sibling, who is sympathetic to the nonwhite one, is haunted by the existence of the other and yet dependent on the subjugation of that other for his/her own self-actualization. The interdependence of these pairs mirrors the codependency of blackness and whiteness in U.S. culture. Cable's novel depends on mixed-race characters not only to outline the complexity of racial prescription but also to protest the perpetuation of racial inequalities. Indeed, the final pairing of a mixed-race woman and a rebellious African slave addresses the possibilities of black liberation. Functioning in answer to the other pairings, the supernatural connection between the African slave, who was tortured and killed eight years before the time of the novel's main plot, and the mixed-race woman who shares his spirit, though not his strength, proclaims the urgency of black liberation.

But ultimately Cable's interpretation of black freedom is gendered, substituting the restoration of black male patriarchy for black civic and social advancement.

George E. Marcus's delineation of the critique of autonomous individualism in late-nineteenth-century American novels offers an illuminating framework within which to consider the paired figures in Cable's novel. Reading these works as responses to the pervasive ideology of the unified self in Euro-American cultural thought, Marcus describes three devices that express disjointed selves in late-nineteenth-century works: divided, doubled, and crossed selves. The divided self is marked by complex internal thought processes, as in psychological novels. Doubled selves demonstrate distinct, dual personalities in a single person. The crossed self exchanges identities with another character, whether through deception or mistake.[1] Marcus concludes that this later critique of the autonomous self is the most effective:

> [C]rossed selves as a tactic of plotting and character development in the nineteenth-century American novel were a powerful chiasmus-like mode for engaging the reader, even if through an unrelenting effect of slight cognitive imbalance, with the subversive truth of the arbitrariness of cultural categories and especially as they apply to a near sacred ideology in American life about autonomous individualism and the coherent self.[2]

Cable's simultaneous expression of difference and the blurring of those boundaries, Marcus contends, defeats the reader's attempt to separate the two figures.

In *The Grandissimes,* Cable's mulatto figures function as both doubled and crossed selves to express the duality of American identity as shaped by race. Indeed, one could argue that mulatto figures are the ultimate embodiment of the doubled self, straddling the margins that divide the nation. Cable highlights this duality by representing his mulatto figures as both slaveholders and victims of slavery and racial exclusion. Their interests in two communities whose wishes are opposed demonstrate their bifurcation. Cable's implementation of the crossed self emerges in his development of the mulatto-white sibling pairs. One pair of the siblings even shares the same name, a situation which ultimately produces much confusion, both mistakenly and purposefully. These racialized crossed selves in *The Grandissimes* are not so much about the problem of the unified self in general as they are about the myth of a unified American identity marked by whiteness. The narrative of crossed selves in Cable's novel is an allegory of the ways in which racial interdiction articulates U.S. identity. The racialized crossed selves demonstrate how whiteness and its privileges ultimately depend on the definition of blackness and the subjugation of those identified as black.

The way in which the representation of doubled and crossed selves explores the impact of race on the national structure in Mark Twain's *Pudd'nhead Wilson* (1894) illuminates the larger implications of Cable's novel. Indeed, one might think of Twain's novel, published fifteen years after Cable's, as one that engages not only Cable's work but a lengthy tradition of mixed-race fiction as well. In his reading of *Pudd'nhead Wilson,* Marcus argues that while one effect of crossed selves is the expression of the arbitrariness of racial categories, race is not so much the subject of *Pudd'nhead Wilson* as it is a vehicle for exploring the damage produced by the combined factors of social classification and the principle of the unified self. He writes, "Race then is merely an occasion for exploring the masked complexities of consciousness and self."[3] In contrast, I argue that Twain's contention with the concept of a unified self had everything to do with the understanding that the notion of self-identity was shaped by the concept of essential racial identities. Thus, while I agree with Marcus that the confused selves in *Pudd'nhead Wilson* serve to destabilize the notion of self-identity, I also contend that Twain's larger goal is to destabilize the concept of race as the fundamental biological building block of self-identity and thus challenge its role as the principal determinant of American civil privileges.

Like Cable, Twain examined the effects of the history of slavery on the post-Reconstruction South through mixed-race characters. *Pudd'nhead Wilson,* the story of a mixed-race woman who switched her child with that of the master to allow him to escape the perils of slavery, confronted the racist ideology that pervaded the United States in 1894, when Twain's novel was first published. As many writers before him had done, Twain employed a literary figure who for many had come to embody the conflictedness of slavery in a nation founded on principles of liberty. Critics such as Stanley Brodwin have pointed out that the Edenic setting in *Pudd'nhead Wilson* highlights Twain's intention to speak to the American condition.[4] As Brodwin notes, *Pudd'nhead Wilson* opens with the Edenic description of Dawson's Landing, whose homes were surrounded by "tangles of rose vines, honey suckles and morning-glories . . . hollyhocks, marigolds, touch-me-nots, princes feathers and other old-fashioned flowers."[5] This lush description is abruptly arrested by the narrative interruption: "Dawson's Landing was a slave-holding town, with a rich slave-worked grain and pork country back of it."[6] This announcement of what lies in "back of" Dawson's Landing highlights the fabrication of American freedom as well as the ways in which that invention relies on human bondage as its definitive antipode.

This coupling of mulattos in Eden occurs frequently in antebellum and postbellum mulatto fiction. This semblance between Twain's and Cable's novels, as well as works such as H. L. Hosmer's *Adela the Octoroon,* Child's "The Quadroons" and *A Romance of the Republic,* W. W. Smith's *The Yankee Slave Driver,* and William Wells Brown's *Clotel,* suggests the way in which mulatto figures in Eden operate as cultural signifiers; it would have recalled the contradiction between a mythologized unified United States and the reality of a nation fragmented by race. Twain's novel disrupts the predominant narrative of American freedom by implying that a counternarrative of bondage undergirds and defines that freedom.[7] His text evokes the myth of America to trace the end of the metaphorical Eden and the culprit, the national sin of slavery. But unlike prewar mulatto fiction, Twain's recollection of slavery points to both the institution of slavery and the reinstitutionalization of racism in the 1880s and 1890s, as Shelly Fisher Fishkin has pointed out.[8] Indeed, that Dawson's Landing is a new town only fifty years old and Twain's story is published only thirty-three years after emancipation suggests a self-conscious retrospective moment. By paralleling antebellum slavery with a supposedly newly reconstructed America, Twain revises the mulatto-in-Eden configuration to consider the failure of Reconstruction.

The exploration of doubled and crossed selves within the context of mulattos in Eden suggests the ways in which the concept of race bifurcates national identity, matching freedom with slavery, defining white privilege through the subjugation of blacks. As in Cable's novel, the doubled and crossed selves that emerge in Twain's *Pudd'nhead Wilson* are mulatto figures. As Marcus points out, Twain's Roxy suggests the doubled self because of the disassociation between her body and her racial identity.[9] Likewise, the switching of Tom and Chambers enacts crossed selves that problematize the reliability of racial categories and, I would argue, points to the myth of a unified American identity constructed as essentially white. In comparison, Cable's *The Grandissimes* also relies on doubled and crossed selves not only to destabilize racial bifurcation but also to expose whiteness as a concept utterly dependent on the notion of blackness. By situating his German-American protagonist as incapable of distinguishing between two brothers, one defined as white, the other as black, Cable elicits confusion that penetrates the fabrication of these categories so central to American culture. The pairing of a slave woman and her half-sibling mistress becomes another means through which Cable explores the interconstructedness of blackness and whiteness, but in this case through the conscious lens of gender. Considering the cultural limitations placed on white women, as well as their social advantages over nonwhite women, Cable illuminates complex intersections between race and gender. In addition, by pairing a quadroon woman with both her white sibling figure and a rebellious African slave, Cable builds a device that elicits both queries and solutions concerning the problem of the color line in the United States. This sequence of pairs performs in two ways. First, by pairing the quadroon woman with both slave and mistress, Cable punctuates her transformation from slave to mistress. Her transformation asks the question, If the goal of a freed slave is to become the slaveholder, how can the stronghold of slavery ever be broken? Second, by pairing the quadroon woman with two crossed selves, her white mistress and a deceased African slave, Cable invites a consideration of gender roles in relationship to racial prescription. More expressly, by casting the quadroon woman's aggression as similar to that of her murdered black male peer and divergent from the passivity of her white mistress, Cable creates a reversal of traditional gender roles that stems from the emasculation of black men. While this portrayal considers the sexual exploitation of black women, ultimately the subject of black liberation is black men, whose degradation functions as the definitive vehicle of racial oppression in the novel.

The Grandissimes

Examining the history of slavery was not new to George Washington Cable. His early short story "Tité Poulette" (1874) reflects on the problems of the color line, focusing on a quadroon woman who must deny her daughter to prove that the daughter is white.[10] She does this to allow her daughter to legally marry a white man rather than become a concubine, as she had been. Though this image of maternal denial at once permeates and crystallizes the cultural power of race construction, critics have suggested that the story, with its critique of racism embedded in a romantic saga of forbidden love, only grazes the problem of racial inequality in comparison to Cable's later work.[11] Indeed, in *The Grandissimes,* Cable attempts to address these incendiary issues more directly and in more detail. Considered by many recent critics to be Cable's best novel, *The Grandissimes* was originally published in serial form in *Scribner's Monthly.* The editors at *Scribner's* were not pleased with the novel's overt attention to slavery and racism. They asked Cable to avoid such topics and pressured him to shorten the scenes that included black characters.[12] But Cable resisted and in later years wrote of the novel: "I meant to make *The Grandissimes* as truly a political work as ever it has been called."[13] The harsh criticism that Cable received from his editors and his audience suggests that Cable succeeded in doing just that.

Like Twain's *Pudd'nhead Wilson, The Grandissimes* is set in an earlier period which recalls the present. Published soon after the Compromise of 1877, the novel confronts a social and political climate shaped by the return of political power to the South through a story set in 1803 Louisiana as it passed from French to U.S. control. Using this political shift to discuss the post-Reconstruction age, Cable examines the rejection of democratic ideals both in early Louisiana and in the post-Reconstruction South.[14] Through a series of characters who represent various points of view concerning the American condition, Cable offers a story that dramatizes the nation's racial dilemma after Reconstruction, protesting the perpetuation of American racism. The multiple plots in *The Grandissimes* converge with the novel's protagonist, Joseph Frowenfeld, a German-American immigrant to Louisiana. Dedicated to principles of democracy, Joseph functions as the moral voice of the novel, and critics have suggested that the character is based on Cable, who was also an outsider among the Creole culture of Louisiana.[15] Though initially Joseph is overzealous and fulsomely candid in his criticism of the Creoles, he eventually learns that "you mus' *crack* the egg, not smash it!"[16] Joseph functions as the prototypical northerner who must learn that he cannot force the South to change and that condescension will only produce alienation from the community with which he must live. Through polite but honest debate, Joseph is able to revive the spirit of democracy in the dashing Honoré Grandissime, the most honored member of the illustrious and enormous Grandissime clan. Educated in Paris, Honoré, since his return, had comfortably reverted to acceptance of Creole prejudice. His renewed liberal views on race recall the hope of the New South and a willingness to change with changing times. In contrast, his stodgy uncle, Agricola Fusilier, maintains his aristocratic views and insists upon the separation of the races and opposition to American government. Agricola's dedication to the old regime, which culminates in his deathbed affirmation of racial segregation, suggests the disinclination of southerners to relinquish the old South and its patrician and racist ideas.

Despite the neatness of this allegory of regional and generational conflict, Cable introduces a complex series of crossed selves that complicate the story's narrative scope. The most obvious image of crossed selves in the book consists of Honoré Grandissime and his older half-brother, who bears the same name; the only distinction is the addition of the abbreviation "f.m.c.," signifying free man of color. Honoré Grandissime f.m.c. is the child of a quadroon woman and Numa Grandissime, the father that the two men share. Educated in Paris alongside his brother, Honoré f.m.c. inherited the larger share of their father's assets. He becomes a rentier and slaveholder, and though he is nearly white, he must contend with the prejudice of the Creole community, most of which hold similar views to Agricola. As Lawrence Berkov has pointed out, Honoré f.m.c. functions as a vehicle to represent the sham freedom that freed people were experiencing after the war.[17] Like the freed people, Honoré f.m.c. believes he is not a slave, and yet his freedom is restricted severely by both law and custom.

Cable introduces another mixed-race character, the beautiful Palmyre Philosophe. Like Honoré f.m.c., Palmyre functions as counterpart to a white sibling figure, Aurora De Grapion. The nearly white slave of a rival family of the Grandissimes, the De Grapion clan, Palmyre as a child is given to the young Aurora De Grapion for a waiting maid, and the two youngsters develop an affectionate sisterly relationship. Indeed, the text implies that the girls are half-siblings.[18] But their life together ends when Palmyre is subsequently taken away because the De Grapions feel that her "ruling spirit" threatens to reverse the mistress-slave relationship.[19] She is loaned to the Grandissimes, who try to buy her, but the De Grapion family, for the sake of honor (not wanting to appear as though they need the money) insist on keeping ownership of her. From her youth she falls hopelessly in love with the white Honoré, just as Honoré f.m.c. is desperately in love with her. Her love for Honoré is matched only by her passionate desire to kill Agricola, the symbol of white southern racist beliefs. Their hatred is mutual; Agricola despises Palmyre for having the pride to love a Grandissime, but because he fears her purported occult powers he has her freed.

Cable complicates the doubling between Palmyre and Aurora by also pairing Palmyre with a slave called Bras Coupé. Much of Palmyre's characterization depends on her relationship to Bras Coupé, a slave killed eight years before the time of the story. Brought directly from Africa, Bras Coupé is a proud prince who is purchased by Agricola, who notices his great beauty. Agricola sells him to his sister's fiancé, Jose Martinez. When Bras Coupé strikes the overseer and refuses to do menial labor, Martinez, who admires his courage, sends for a translator, Palmyre. Bras Coupé agrees to work only if Palmyre will be his wife. Martinez and Agricola decide that she will marry him, despite her initial opposition to the scheme. Later, she consents to marry him to advance her plan to have him lead a slave insurrection as revenge against Agricola. But at the wedding, Bras Coupé gets drunk, demands more alcohol of Martinez, and then strikes him "in self-defense."[20]

Bras Coupé escapes to the swamp and puts a curse on Martinez that destroys his plantation. Later, when Bras Coupé is captured, Martinez and Agricola show him no mercy. Bras Coupé's ears are cut off, his hamstrings are severed, and he is flogged. Palmyre attends him faithfully, and before he dies, she has the mistress bring her baby to him so that he can lift the curse that has by then killed Martinez. The connection between Palmyre and Bras Coupé is primarily a supernatural one; Palmyre becomes the vessel through which the haunting spirit of the mutilated man lives on. As one onlooker puts it, Bras Coupé's "spirit has gone into Palmyre."[21] The story of Bras Coupé is told by numerous characters whose purposes range, as Suzanne Jones argues, from a desire to affect social change to the expression of the impossibility of affecting such change.[22] It becomes the soul of Cable's story because it addresses the black codes of Louisiana and the Jim Crow laws of Cable's time and encapsulates the undeniable violence against blacks that was mounting during the post-Reconstruction era. Because the story is in some way related to each of the characters, it demonstrates how the shadow of slavery, or what Frowenfeld calls "the shadow of the Ethiopian," constantly hovers over the American nation.[23]

Doubles in Eden

Cable develops the image of Eden after the fall as the context for these crossed selves. Cable's Eden is a ghastly, corroded landscape. Frowenfeld arrives in Louisiana for the first time expecting "bright visions, anticipations of verdure, and fragrance, and tropical gorgeousness"; instead, he finds "a land hung in mourning, darkened by gigantic cypresses, submerged; a land of reptiles, silence, shadow, decay."[24] Trying to fight disappointment, Frowenfeld says, "[W]hat the Creator had pronounced very good they could hardly feel free to condemn."[25] Joseph's father notes that the scene reminded him of the "half-built world," what the narrator calls "the panorama of creation—before the earth was ready for the dog's master."[26] In its incompleteness and grotesque deformity, Cable's Eden recalls the failure of Reconstruction and the "half-built" nation left in its wake.

The crux of Cable's exploration of the nation's social failings lies in his depiction of the caste system that results in the twining of families and siblings in the book. According to Stephanie Foote, this series of racial and historical doubles "embody the hidden genealogy of Creole culture."[27] Indeed, the unearthing of this genealogy consumes the first 100 pages of the novel, until the baffling problem of the two Honorés is finally explained. Frowenfeld and other newcomers mistake Honoré f.m.c. for his half-brother. Indeed, Honoré f.m.c. encourages the error by occasionally omitting the suffix that denotes his racial background when he signs his name. While Cable's portrayal of this confusion implies the arbitrariness of racial constructions that deem one brother white and another black, this misunderstanding also expresses the ways in which the differentiation between the two Honorés depends on the existence of the other. That is, the identity of the white Honoré, who is revered as the most honored member of the ruling class, depends on the subjugation and alienation of his brother, who is deemed a member of the underclass. All the social trappings that make Honoré the revered leader of the most respected Creole family clan, his political authority and social influence, depend not merely on his family name and wealth, both of which are shared by his nonwhite half-brother, but on his whiteness, which demands his participation in the social alienation and public humiliation of his brother. While the two men are studying in France, Honoré assumes a familiarity with Honoré f.m.c. But when the men return to Louisiana, Honoré reverts to the prejudices of Creole society and shuns his brother. Honoré's resumption of his role as honored citizen depends on his relinquishing social equality with his brother. This relapse indicates the centrality of race in the formulation of Creole culture and government and its referent, the American nation.

Honoré's explanation for why he submits to the prejudices of his fellow Creoles clarifies how his position within the community depends on this conformity: "[T]he water must expect to take the shape of the bucket."[28] Cable represents Honoré as aware not only of this contingency but also of the larger implications of this interdependence of whiteness and blackness within the culture. In a discussion of racial caste, Honoré expresses to Frowenfeld the ways in which race pierces the culture:

> It is the *Némésis* w'ich, instead of coming afteh, glides along by the side of this morhal, political, commercial, social mistake! It blanches . . . ow whole civilization! It drhags us a centurhy behind the rhes' of the world! It rhetahds and poisons everhy industrhy we got!—mos' of all our-h immense agrhiculture! It brheeds a thousan' cusses that nevva leave home but jus flutter-h up an' rhoost . . . on ow *heads;* an' we nevva know it!—yes, sometimes some of us know it.[29]

As he argues that racial division shapes the philosophical, political, social, and economic workings of the culture, Honoré's final image of a culture that breeds offspring as a lingering reminder of its social wrongs insinuates his own familial relationship to his brother. Driving home this connection, Frowenfeld interrupts, declaring this cultural phenomenon "the shadow of the Ethiopian."[30] Likewise, the narrator often refers to Honoré f.m.c. as a "shadow," highlighting these parallels between blackness and whiteness and Honoré and his brother. The confusion over which brother is which and the way in which the clarification of their identities demands the reference to the other suggest the mutual dependence of their identities. Honoré is identified as the white Honoré because his brother is considered the black one and vice versa.

Despite the ways in which the two men are forever yoked, Honoré f.m.c. sinks under the problems of caste that elevate Honoré. The very conditions that establish Honoré as a leader among the Creoles serve to exclude Honoré f.m.c. from Creole culture. The social structure that produces the gallant Honoré shapes Honoré f.m.c. into a meek, passive, doleful, and suicidal figure. A strikingly handsome man capable of passing for white, Honoré f.m.c. resents his social position and longs for Palmyre, who does not return his love. Even this unrequited love for Palmyre, which eventually proves fatal, is involuntarily determined by Honoré, whom Palmyre chooses over his brother. The construction of this love triangle reinscribes the connectedness of the men's fates; each of Honoré's advantages result in the disadvantage of his brother. The most striking example of this, however, is when Honoré accepts a proposal from his brother to become his business partner as a gesture of restitution. In exchange for the support of his brother's fortune, Honoré agrees to rename his mercantile firm The Grandissime Brothers. Ultimately, Honoré's attempt at reparation benefits him more than his brother. His brother's fortune saves Honoré from bankruptcy, but Honoré f.m.c.'s social humiliation and romantic rejection continue, finally resulting in his suicide.

This image of crossed selves, one perpetually condemned by the other's privileges, suggests the ineffectualness of a single well-meaning white man's actions against the prevailing system of racial prejudice. Cable's treatment of Honoré f.m.c. also indicates solutions that might erupt from black and mixed-race communities. Cable elucidates a course of action to address the problem of racial division through Frowenfeld, who preaches to Honoré f.m.c. about his duty to protest racism. Insisting on the similarity between slaves and free people of color, Frowenfeld explains that a man in Honoré f.m.c.'s situation might be able to stir free blacks to a "noble discontent, laying out his means . . . for their enlightenment, their moral elevation, their training in skilled work."[31] Finally, he encourages him to go among fair-minded whites, "seeking to prevail with them for a public recognition of the rights of all."[32] Cable's ability to imagine black leaders who would peacefully and successfully protest American racism is a bold assertion that anticipates the Civil Rights Movement. In addition, Frowenfeld's insistence on the connections between the condition of free people of color and slaves declares the importance of historicity in determining the course of social protest among freed blacks. Cable's positioning of Frowenfeld as duty bound to awaken these easily contented blacks is nothing less than patronizing. As Frowenfeld declares that such blacks are "a warning to philanthropists," Cable imparts the impatience with black progress that contributed to the end of Reconstruction efforts.[33] Frowenfeld's role as the overseer of this call to action reveals the limitations of Cable's representation of black leadership in the struggle for black equality.

Honoré f.m.c. never carries out Frowenfeld's directive; instead, he murders Agricola, his half-brother's uncle. The murder expresses the inadequacy of violence in addressing the complicated social, historical, and biological ties that penetrate the color line. The scene which initiates the murder conveys the desire of Creoles to suppress the history of cross-racial contact despite the presence of the sign of interracial history—the mixed-race individual. Agricola's murder follows his declaration of the solidity of the color line in Creole culture. As Agricola explains to the men in Frowenfeld's shop that a black woman slave accused of plotting to murder him by voodoo would not be treated the same as a white person accused of the same crime, he is interrupted by "a shadow approaching from the door."[34] Honoré f.m.c., the shadow cast by Creole indulgence, exploitative customs, and oppressive regimes, enters and Agricola humiliates him, demanding that he remove his hat in the presence of the whites and insisting that Frowenfeld eject him from the shop. Agricola's wish to expel him demonstrates the desire to exclude the complicated history of race relations that produced Honoré f.m.c. As Agricola puts it, "h-tradition is much more authentic than history!"[35] When Agricola attacks him, Honoré f.m.c. stabs him, mortally wounding him. Cable orchestrates this scene so that the only site where Honoré f.m.c. can place the wound is in Agricola's back. Thus, he kills his near-kinsman (the brother of his father's legal wife) by stabbing him in the back in response to a frontal attack. While the scene reflects the growing tide of violence against blacks as a motive for black reprisal, the presence of the double also marks the futility of the attempts of both men to destroy the complicated familial and cultural ties that bind the twinned families. Honoré f.m.c.'s entrance into the shop as a social equal and Agricola's subsequent attempt to humble him represent the social choices available to the

New South—to accept social equality or fight it, hanging on desperately to tradition until the conflict leads to self-destruction. But in Cable's imagination, violence is ultimately ineffectual. The murder of Agricola does not change Honoré f.m.c.'s sad condition. Indeed, it forces him to flee to France with Palmyre, whose indifference toward him continues.

The Serpent in the Garden

Marked by her relationship to her white sibling figure Aurora as well as her spiritual kinship with the dead rebellious slave Bras Coupé, Palmyre is by far the more dynamic of the two mixed-race characters in the novel. Possessing the beauty, charm, and chastity of Aurora, Palmyre is also cunning, vengeful, and fierce, like Bras Coupé. Cable's descriptions of her are rife with perplexing conflicts:

> [T]he faint red tinge that blushed with a kind of cold passion through the clear yellow skin of the cheek, the fullness of the red, voluptuous lips and the roundness of her perfect neck, gave her, even at fourteen a barbaric and magnetic beauty, that startled the beholder like an unexpected drawing out of a jeweled sword. Such a type could have sprung only from high Latin ancestry on the one side and . . . Jaloff African on the other. To these charms of person she added mental acuteness, conversational adroitness, concealed cunning and noiseless but visible strength of will; and to these, that rarest of gifts in one of her tincture, the purity of true womanhood.[36]

The passage captures the sense of contradiction that Anna Shannon Elfenbein calls "chilling paradoxes—a familiar racist way of perceiving mixed-race characters."[37] Cable exploits this convention to position Palmyre as the product of a nation divided. Riddled with inner contradiction, Palmyre functions as a readable boundary between the castes. That is, Palmyre's doubleness highlights her role as the site of cultural, historical, social, and political conflict in the United States. Bearing both the history of the De Grapions and that of Bras Coupé, she compels the comparison of these conflicted histories and highlights their interrelationship.

Like the filial relationship between the two Honorés, the relationship between Palmyre and Aurora also explores the interdependence of blackness and whiteness in the construction of American cultural identity. The separation of these sibling figures by cultural barriers that demand Palmyre's submission as a slave and Aurora's dominance as mistress captures the crux of this interdependence. This plot recalls the way in which the mixed-race maternal figure's sacrifice of her daughter in Cable's "Tité Poulette" captures the power of race construction over domestic lives. But unlike the maternal figure in Cable's "Tité Poulette," who sacrifices her biological tie to her daughter, Palmyre's relation to her sister figure, Aurora, is never overtly revealed. While the sisterly affection between the two women is apparent, the circumstances through which Palmyre became "one who *shared the blood of the De Grapions*" is left to conjecture.[38] Because it is Aurora's father who threatens to kill anyone who dares to dishonor Palmyre by permitting the African Bras Coupé to marry her, the reader is left to assume that he is the father of Palmyre. This construction of Palmyre in relation to the De Grapions and Bras Coupé demonstrates the complexity of her position. The De Grapions expel her from their family because she fails to assume a submissive posture in relation to them, and yet they claim her honor as a reflection of their own and seek to prevent her connection to Bras Coupé, demonstrating the tangled interdependence of black and white identities. Through the formation of Palmyre's two crossed selves, Cable elucidates the complexity of Palmyre's cultural, social, and historical position.

In many ways, Cable's treatment of the relationship between Aurora and Palmyre is more complex than his treatment of the brothers because while it considers how these women's lives are shaped by racial categories, it also expresses the social restrictions placed on white women. The mixed-race character functions as the more aggressive of the two women, while the white woman is presented as a passive figure. In this aspect, Cable's characterization seems to rely on common perceptions of white and black womanhood by representing the dependency and susceptibility of the white female figure and the self-sufficiency and resilience of the woman of African descent. Cable's representation of Aurora, however, addresses the problems of middle-class white women's financial dependence on men. Left without a fortune because her late husband gambled away their property, Aurora and her daughter, Clotilde, are nearly penniless and unable to pay their rent. Their debt to their landlord, Honoré f.m.c., grows as they seek other means of procuring the money without working. As Clotilde puts it, "[W]hat troubles us is not how to make a living, but how to get a living without making it."[39] Aurora explains that society demands that they not work, because if women could earn their own living they would never marry. Aurora and Clotilde are reduced to seeking the sympathy and aid of the two mixed-raced characters in the novel, Honoré f.m.c. and Palmyre, whom Aurora approaches once to seek a spell to acquire money and again in search of a love potion to attract Honoré. This image of their poverty in relation to the financial independence of Honoré f.m.c. and Palmyre indicates the severe limitations placed on white women, whose only choice seems to be to marry.

Yet Cable complicates this representation by developing a paradigm in which the white character, despite her passivity and frailty, benefits romantically and financially from the social exclusion of her sibling figure. Though both women are honorable, faithful, and beautiful, because of the racially imprinted constructions of women, Aurora's social role is that of a lady worthy of financial support, thus demanding her exclusion from the labor market, while Palmyre is a woman unworthy of honorable love, requiring that she support herself. Palmyre's financial independence, her contact with the commercial world, is not only required of her, it also marks her as vulnerable to the dangers of the marketplace because she too is considered nothing more than a commodity, what the narrator describes as "legitimate prey."[40] Despite her status as free, Palmyre's sexual vulnerability frames her as a temptation. Aurora's freedom to obtain honorable love and Palmyre's inability to inspire more than lust or contempt shapes their conjoined fates: one's advantages seals the other's doom.

The complicated love plot that entangles these women reveals how Palmyre's exclusion profits Aurora. From the beginning, Palmyre's love for Honoré is doomed to remain unreciprocated because the freedom to marry a white man, to participate in public intercourse as a social equal, are privileges that Palmyre lacks. Aware of her interest in him, Honoré steadfastly avoids her for the sake of his honor. As a result, there is not a single scene in the novel in which they converse. Palmyre, unaware that Aurora also loves Honoré, attempts to aid Aurora by giving her a love charm to lure him. Thus, not only is her loss Aurora's gain, but she unwittingly attempts to maintain this imbalance. Aurora and Honoré are united, while Palmyre and Honoré f.m.c. must flee New Orleans.

These antithetical projected roles entrap both women, one's honor demanding the other's dishonor. Cable's love plot demonstrates how the construction of Palmyre as sexually available despite her purity determines her vulnerability to sexual exploitation. Palmyre's exposure poses a dangerous temptation for even the most honorable of men. Unmarriageable to a white man, Palmyre is considered sexually available to anyone. While Honoré never speaks directly about why he avoids Palmyre, his advice to Frowenfeld to do the same and Frowenfeld's subsequent encounters with Palmyre clarify the sexual threat that she poses. Recovering from a gunshot wound that she receives in her violent attempt on Agricola's life, Palmyre is treated by Frowenfeld while the doctor is sick. When Frowenfeld explains that he has been visiting Palmyre's home for this purpose, Honoré cautions him that if he does not seek another arrangement, he will be subject to slander, and he adds that Frowenfeld will find himself "under the 'shadow of the Ethiopian,'" trapped by the complicated racial entanglements born from the history of slavery.[41] Honoré's suggestion that even Frowenfeld, an outsider to the Creole society, might also be lured into a sexual arrangement with a quadroon woman bespeaks the temptation that Palmyre offers.

This threat is better elucidated in Palmyre's encounters with Frowenfeld. Louis Rubin has noted that the scene in which Frowenfeld treats Palmyre's wounds is replete with repressed sexuality. The scene demonstrates the perilous allure of Palmyre's vulnerability.[42] When Frowenfeld attempts to examine and dress her wounded shoulder as she lies in bed, Palmyre meets his attempts with distrust and resistance. Her disbelief in the possibility that a white man could see and touch her body without sexual motivations expresses the social context of sexual exploitation which frames this encounter. While Frowenfeld's "womanly touch" and "commanding gentleness . . . inspired Palmyre with . . . a sense of safety," his attraction to her and the danger of this attraction is communicated through the scene's beginning.[43] When Frowenfeld arrives, he gazes into the fire before his eyes meet Palmyre's hostile ones. Frowenfeld reflects on the source of her resentment:

> This monument of the shame of two races—this poisonous blossom of crime growing out of crime—this final, unanswerable white man's accuser—this would-be murderess—what ranks and companies would have to stand up in the Great Day with her and answer as accessory before the fact![44]

Bearing the weight of history, Palmyre stands as testament to the sins of the past, evidence of the men who failed to resist temptation. He concludes this reflection by gazing again into the fire, the symbol of his own temptation and rebuke. Though he withdraws without succumbing, many hours would pass "before he could replace with more tranquillizing images the vision of the philosophe [Palmyre] reclining among her pillows."[45] Later, Frowenfeld concludes that despite his principles, he will surrender to this attraction if he continues to come into contact with Palmyre. This inner conflict surfaces later in the novel when Palmyre grabs his hand, begging Frowenfeld to give her a charm to entice Honoré. Frowenfeld recognizes that her touch "to him, was poisonous" and "the better man in him was suffocating."[46] The intensity of Frowenfeld's predicament escalates, until he "scarce [has] power left to liberate his right hand with his left, to seize his hat and go."[47] Finally, Palmyre drops to her knees, "her arms bared of their drapery."[48] The reader never knows whether or not Frowenfeld would have succumbed, because Palmyre's slave woman hits him over the head suddenly, believing that he must be harming her mistress.

What is fascinating about Frowenfeld's temptation is that Palmyre is not begging for his love but rather for his assistance in attracting Honoré. Her shameless desire for the affection of a man who can never legally marry her, however, is enough to indicate her sexual susceptibility and thus inveigle Frowenfeld. This representation of Frowenfeld's encounter with Palmyre as a battle for his soul fetishizes Palmyre's sexual vulnerability and ultimately her blackness, the root of that susceptibility. That is, because Palmyre does not have the legitimacy that whiteness would afford, she is vulnerable to sexual exploitation, and therefore her blackness condemns her to the role of temptress. It is odd that her sexual susceptibility is positioned as an active force within the novel, capable of steering well-intentioned, principled men, such as Frowenfeld, from their course. Palmyre's susceptibility to abuse becomes the unlikely source of her power over the white men in the novel because her exposure initiates their moral degradation. Her table, its legs made of "upward-writhing images of three scaly serpents," mirrors her role as the tempting serpent in the garden.[49] Cable expresses the interrelationship between the races problematically by situating the dilemma of black women's vulnerability to sexual exploitation as a threat to the integrity of white men.[50]

But as with all of Palmyre's defining characteristics, her vulnerability is matched by its opposite, animalistic ferocity. Palmyre, the ultimate doubled self, despite her vulnerability, is described as a feral creature requiring restraint:

> That barbaric beauty which had begun to bud twenty years before was now in perfect bloom. The united grace and pride of her movement was inspiring but—what shall we say?—feline? It was femininity without humanity,—something that made her with all her superbness, a creature that one would want to find chained.[51]

James Frisby has said of this passage that it is as sexual as any American writer of the period could present and that the author "wishes he had the chains," indicating that the scene represents Cable's personal fantasy.[52] This use of sadistic portrayals in depictions of mulatto figures, however, was not new or singular to Cable. In fact, as Elfenbein has noted, bondage images pervaded antebellum mulatto fiction, titillating audiences with illustrations of helpless women in manacles exposed to the debased imaginations of villains and voyeuristic readers. However, she considers this interpretation of Cable's description of Palmyre as a misreading of both Cable and Palmyre. She reads this scene as consciously calculated to show Frowenfeld's "Latin view of the quadroon" as well as Palmyre's "vulnerability and her need to be accepted as a human being, despite her hostile pose."[53] In contrast, I argue that the challenge that Cable poses to Palmyre's humanity and the threat that she poses to the morality of the white male characters serve to justify this bondage scenario.

Cable's repetition of this simultaneously racist and sexist portrayal seems incongruent with the novel's expression of sympathy for the black condition. Indeed, the image of Palmyre's bondage in the context of a novel that professes to support black freedom indicates the gendered interpretation of black liberation in the novel. It is Honoré f.m.c. whom Frowenfeld encourages to arouse discontent among the black masses, despite Honoré f.m.c.'s "feeble will (the trait of his caste)."[54] Frowenfeld's belief that a race leader must be male is not surprising. But the juxtaposition that Cable frames between Palmyre's bestial thirst for violence and Honoré f.m.c.'s faint resolve suggests that male leadership might check aggressive women such as Palmyre. As John Clemen notes, Cable depicts Honoré f.m.c.'s passivity and Palmyre's ruthlessness as a reversal of gender roles.[55] This exchange of social roles spawns the larger problem of Palmyre's sexual vulnerability. Palmyre requires restraint and protection, which ideally would be provided by a man of her own caste who would act on her behalf. Honoré f.m.c.'s passivity allows for Palmyre's sexual availability, which theoretically leads to the moral temptation of white men. Frowenfeld, speaking of free people of color, states the problem thus:

> Your men, for a little property, and your women, for a little amorous attention, let themselves be shorn even of the virtue of discontent, and for a paltry bait of sham freedom have consented to endure a tyrannous contumely which flattens them into the dirt like grass under a slab.[56]

This`1` reading of free people of color mirrors the actions of Honoré f.m.c. and Palmyre. Satisfied with being a successful businessman, Honoré f.m.c. actively manages his inheritance while he passively suffers a longing for Palmyre. In turn, Palmyre is consumed by a desire to satisfy her passion for two men—her love for Honoré and her hatred of Agricola.[57] When coupled with his gendered statement of the errors of the free people of color, Frowenfeld's suggestion that Honoré f.m.c. become a race leader implies the necessity of patriarchy.

Palmyre's affinity with the dead slave Bras Coupé confirms that her aggression is sparked by the failure of men such as Honoré f.m.c. to advocate on her behalf. Though she never loves Bras Coupé because her heart already belongs to Honoré, she ardently admires the rebellious slave and sees in him "the gigantic embodiment of her own dark, fierce will, the expanded realization of her lifetime longing for terrible strength."[58] By depicting her dedication to him as the result of Bras Coupé's profound heroism and stern resolve, Cable suggests that Honoré f.m.c.'s passivity about the racism of the Creoles is the source of Palmyre's seething rage. Her eagerness to allow Bras Coupé to strike out against the Creoles on her behalf demonstrates her willingness to show deference to a courageous man. This portrayal of the brave Palmyre seeing the fulfillment of her need for a masculine champion in the African indicates the ways in which the novel positions black liberation as the restoration of black male patriarchy.

Ultimately, this pairing of Palmyre and Bras Coupé introduces the larger problem that Cable grapples with throughout the novel: the sexual power that Bras Coupé's bravery, beauty, and blackness introduce into the novel. Cable's attempt to temper this characterization by having Bras Coupé worship white women as gods (he prostrates himself in the presence of his mistress) only clarifies the sexual threat that he poses. Presenting the pairing of Palmyre and Bras Coupé as supernatural functions as the central solution to this problem in the novel: Bras Coupé can only exist in the past, while Palmyre embodies his spirit in the novel's present. As Bras Coupé's double, Palmyre functions as an inadequate stand-in for black male resistance; Cable thus deflects the sexual virility that Bras Coupé introduces into the novel. The death of his body and the passing of his spirit into the body of a woman allowed Cable to consider the spirit of reprisal without exploring black male aggression, sexual or otherwise. Palmyre's failed attempts to kill Agricola and her acknowledgment of her own physical weakness in leading an uprising demonstrate the effacement of the physical threat that Bras Coupé posed. By locating Palmyre as the present embodiment of Bras Coupé's beauty and rebellion, Cable averts the violent and sexual possibilities that Bras Coupé introduces, focusing instead on Palmyre as the tempting prey rather than the sexual aggressor.

The supernatural relationship between Palmyre and Bras Coupé situates Palmyre as the return of the repressed. Palmyre intersects with most of the novel's gothic elements: doubles, occult practices, and sexualized bondage scenarios. Ultimately, this intersection constructs Palmyre as a vessel through which to consider the burdens of past sins. Surrounded by a series of conflicted layers, Palmyre at her core is the spirit of the dead man. This depiction serves to dehumanize her, situating her as the frightening product of past wrongs and indulgences. In contrast, Bras Coupé's humanity, for all his noble savagery, remains intact through Cable's dramatizations of his humiliation, suffering, and righteous retribution. Indeed, his romanticized fondness for white women, who he exempts from his curse, illustrates his compassion. Palmyre's humanity seems not only extraneous but in opposition to the traditional gender codes embedded in the novel. Her desire to be Bras Coupé signifies her deviance. Cable's descriptions of her elicit a combination of voyeuristic curiosity and fear rather than compassion. The sense of mystery that surrounds her projects her as an object which, despite its vulnerabilities, must be feared. As the embodiment of a dead man, Palmyre is the terrifying vessel of the undead that lives on beyond the life of the novel.

While two of the novel's love plots end happily with the unions of Frowenfeld and Clotilde and Honoré and Aurora, Palmyre and Honoré f.m.c. end sadly with Palmyre still pining for Honoré and Honoré f.m.c.'s unrequited love provoking his suicide. In this sense, Palmyre reflects the free black community that Cable imagines, women of color longing for the amorous attention of white men. However, by denying the romantic expectations for this plot, Cable evokes not only the complicated situation of the free blacks of his own era, whose problems would also not be solved so easily, but also the failures of this "half-built world" that he creates.[59] Cable offers a final image of this failed Eden: "[A] spot where the fallen dead bodies of trees overlay one another and a dense growth of willows and vines and dwarf palmetto shut out the light of the open fields."[60] This passage precedes the slave woman Clemence's lynching, the violent end which Honoré f.m.c. and Palmyre flee to France to escape. Though Cable's portrayal of Palmyre implies that she is the serpent in the garden, Cable's use of nature imagery suggests that perhaps Palmyre is only a branch on a much larger tree of forbidden fruit that first grew from the seeds of slavery. The sense of death and loss that the passage evokes illustrates the failure of Reconstruction and the disintegration of the dream of an egalitarian nation.

In the fifteen years that passed between the publication of *The Grandissimes* and *Pudd'nhead Wilson,* the problems of the color line that divided the nation only worsened. These texts and others demonstrate how mulatto figures became increasingly prevalent in literature with this trend. As the institutionalization of racism came to replace slavery, mulatto characters demonstrated how the roots of American racism had yet to be eliminated in what was supposed to have been a new nation. Mulatto figures allowed these writers to trace the historical discrepancy between the ideology of racial classification and the nation's premise of egalitarianism in order to illustrate the replication of this contradiction in their own times. The sense of the nation's failure that emerges in these works reveals the difficult struggle that would accompany the realization of a new democratic nation. As Honoré puts it: "There are but two steps to civilization, the first easy, the second difficult; to construct—to reconstruct—ah! there it is! the tearing down!"[61]

5

"I will gladly share with them my richer heritage": Schoolteachers in Frances E. W. Harper's *Iola Leroy* and Charles Chesnutt's *Mandy Oxendine*

While George Washington Cable's treatment of mixed-race characters suggests that black communities might become forceful agents of change, the work of African-American writers during the post-Reconstruction age more thoroughly addresses the function of black activism in challenging racial classification in the United States. Frances E. W. Harper's *Iola Leroy,* published in 1892, and Charles Chesnutt's *Mandy Oxendine,* believed to have been written between 1893 and 1896 though it was not published until 1997, engage mixed-race characters to consider the problem of racial classification and the function of African Americans in challenging the authority of racial inequity.[1] That the experience of these mixed-race characters as they straddle the color line is represented not so much as a negotiation of their relationship to whites as it is a negotiation of their relationship to African-American communities indicates the concern of these writers with African-American responses to the widening racial boundaries that characterized the United States at the turn of the century. If works such as Cable's consider "the shadow of the Ethiopian," then texts such as Harper's and Chesnutt's give voice to the shadows; they are "shadows uplifted," as Harper's subtitle reads. Both *Iola Leroy* and *Mandy Oxendine* reflect on the roles of black leaders in the age of self-uplift by situating their mixed-race characters as black schoolteacher figures. The portrayal of teachers in these texts engages conversations about the historical role of black teachers as agents of the self-uplift movement and the direction of African-American communities. The two offer divergent views on the potential roles of black teachers. Harper's text promotes education as a means of moral and political improvement for black people and teachers as a part of the forefront of that movement. In contrast, Chesnutt's novel highlights the cultural distance that education, class, and color can create between a teacher and the black community in which he teaches, challenging the notion of representative black leaders.

Harper's and Chesnutt's portrayal of schoolteacher figures as nearly white complicates the implications of their texts. By combining the figure of a black schoolteacher with a mulatto character, both writers highlight the tension between communal duty and personal ambition, the very conflict that self-uplift ideology posed to middle-class African Americans. Because the mixed-race figure has the option to pass as white and abandon collective interests entirely, he or she functions as the ultimate symbol of this friction. The choice to become a schoolteacher, a symbol of black leadership, evokes the decisive moment in choosing between these paths. The merging of teacher and mulatto figure enables an exploration of self and communal desire. For Harper, the pairing demonstrates that the purpose of self-improvement is to contribute to community advancement. In contrast, Chesnutt challenges the notion of an interdependent community in which individual and shared interests intersect in a uniformly negotiable terrain. Indeed, he disputes the very idea of a knowable monolithic black community whose needs can be assessed and gratified by paradigmatic black leaders.

Schooling the Race

Harper's and Chesnutt's depiction of mulatto figures as teachers reflects the legacy of education as an integral part of black resistance and self-help movements in the nineteenth century. In an essay entitled "A Factor in Human Progress," Harper characterizes the role of education within community service movements:

> The education of the intellect and the training of the morals should go hand-in-hand. The devising brain and the feeling heart should never be divorced, and the question worth asking is not simply, What will education do for us? But, what will it help us to do for others?[2]

When Harper published this essay in the *African Methodist Episcopal Church Review* in 1885, many African Americans were looking to education to solve the problems of African-American communities. As Reconstruction failed, the hostile atmosphere of exploitative work conditions, disenfranchisement, segregation, and growing violence led many blacks to look to internal development in the form of various mutual aid societies, businessmen's organizations, fraternal societies, women's clubs, and church-sponsored social support groups to improve the condition of African-American communities.[3] However, as John Hope Franklin and Alfred A. Moss Jr. wrote, "Negroes could be certain of an improved status only in the field of education."[4]

Harper's and Chesnutt's notion of education as a primary means of both self- and communal advancement reflects this sentiment. In *Iola Leroy,* the advantages of a Western education allow the title character to transform from a white proslavery advocate to a black community leader. The daughter of a southern slaveholder, Iola discovers that her mother was his slave and that at his sudden death she too has been sold into slavery. Rescued by Union forces at the urgings of a former slave, Iola soon identifies herself as colored and dedicates herself to the uplift of black people. Though she becomes a nurse for the Union, she vows, "I intend, when this conflict is over, to cast my lot with the freed people as a helper, teacher, and friend."[5] And it is as a teacher that Iola initiates her role as black community activist, speaking at black salons on methods of improving communities through education. Though Chesnutt's protagonist Lowry has different motives for becoming a teacher, his own educational experience is indicative of the popular belief that education would be the key to defeating the ignorance imposed by racial prejudice. After spending his early years in the "atmosphere of intellectual stagnation" in a poor and disenfranchised community of black and mixed-race people, Lowry attends a freed people's school, where, under the guidance of a northern teacher, he develops a "burning desire for a better education, a broader culture and higher life," which leads him on to college.[6] Though Lowry accepts his first job as a teacher not for the sake of racial uplift but because of a pressing need to earn a living, he is a product of educational initiatives that allow him to reimagine his life possibilities despite the racial oppression encircling him.

The conviction that education could help one transcend the effects of racial exclusion was central to the focus of racial uplift on social and political betterment for African Americans. The historical ban on education for black slaves in most slave states had left education forever tied to the definition of freedom for many African Americans. In fact, this concept of education was an extension of black educational movements that predated the

Civil War.[7] Daniel Alexander Payne, a black graduate of black private education, established a school for adult slaves and free black children in South Carolina in 1828.[8] In addition, as early as 1833 a black school managed by an African-American woman had existed, unknown to the slave regime, in Savannah, Georgia. By 1860, at least 5 percent of slaves were literate.[9] Later, the pursuit of education by freed people during the Reconstruction era was a remarkable illustration of the immutable link between education and the quest for liberty. At the end of the war, many black people erected schools and raised money to pay teachers' salaries. In fact, by 1870, blacks had spent over one million dollars on education, independent of outside support, laying the foundation for universal public education.[10] While they appreciated the aid of white benevolent societies, philanthropists, the Freedmen's Bureau, and state governments, blacks were already organizing schools before any of these groups became involved.[11]

For many African Americans, education was a vital phase of political agitation. As James D. Anderson has pointed out, many black educators believed that "education could help raise the freed people to an appreciation of their historic responsibility to develop a better society and that any significant reorganization of the southern political economy was indissolubly linked to their education."[12] Within this context, black schooling also meant a redefinition of the roles of schoolteachers. If education was to be an integral part of black political advancement, then schoolteachers would be the vanguard of this movement. Implicit in this understanding of education was a belief that black schoolteachers had a responsibility to help blacks to not only help themselves but to help them become a part of the cycle of community uplift to help others.

Because of this interpretation of education as a means of community empowerment, African-American teachers were often viewed as community leaders. In *Iola Leroy,* the fact that the nearly white title character has lived most of her life as white is secondary to her dedication to serving the black community as a black teacher. By taking the initiative to establish schools despite white opposition, risking their own safety in the name of education, many black schoolteachers demonstrated their commitment to black progress and defined themselves as community activists. Being both black and a teacher had political implications in the nineteenth century. While many black educators assumed the dual initiative of teaching moral and liberal education with the hope of preparing African Americans for equal participation as citizens and future black leadership, they also aided freed blacks in legal disputes, worked in mutual aid societies and black churches, and drafted appeals to the Freedmen's Bureau, state officials, and

Congress. In fact, teaching often led to holding political office. At least seventy black teachers served in state legislatures during the Reconstruction era.[13]

While Harper and Chesnutt were writing these novels, many black teachers were continuing their work as community activists in the South after southern redemption. Between 1880 and 1900, though the number of southern black children of school age increased by 25 percent, the proportion attending public schools fell as planters gained control over the laboring classes and demanded child labor. Nevertheless, black educators continued to teach.[14] The Sabbath school tradition, which Harper portrays in *Iola Leroy,* was a system of weekend, night, and Sunday schools established sporadically in the South and more widely in the North long before the Civil War. Black Sabbath schools (sometimes referred to as Sunday schools) were not limited to religious instruction but rather offered elementary instruction to pupils. The number of these schools continued to grow during the Reconstruction and after the Redemption (the period after 1877 when political control returned to the South). They lasted well into the twentieth century as a source of black education that served those who were unable to attend traditional day schools.[15] By 1885, the African Methodist Episcopal church alone reported that it had 200,000 children in Sunday schools, which offered liberal instruction in addition to instruction with the goal of character development.[16] Black institutions of higher education set initiatives to produce more black teachers; nearly one-third of the black college graduates during the era became teachers.[17]

Because black educators were hailed as leaders, to be a black teacher was to be a representative, a litmus test for the future of the race. Even outside black communities, black teachers were often viewed as specimens to gauge the potential of black Americans. Thomas J. Morgan, a white official in the American Home Baptist Mission society, called African-American teachers "models and examples of what their people can and ought to be."[18] Morgan's statement demonstrates the massive responsibility of African-American teachers not only in terms of their relation to the black community but also as representatives in the eyes of whites.

This concept of black teachers made their pedagogies an intense site of debate about the future of the race because curriculum supposedly reflected a model mission for all blacks. The controversy over liberal versus industrial education offers an example of how teacher training programs for blacks often became sites of contention about the best plan for the entire race. According to Anderson, supporters of both industrial education and liberal education felt that "no system of beliefs could be transmitted to the millions of black schoolchildren except through the ideas and behavior of black teachers."[19] The debate over curriculum turned many teacher training programs into campaigns to infiltrate communities with a particular ideology. The intense controversy surrounding teaching methodology demonstrates the role of teachers as a crucial element within the larger framework of racial-uplift philosophy.[20]

But while this ideology encouraged black advancement and unity, it is a paradox that it also thrived on class differences among African Americans. As Kevin Gaines has pointed out, many elite blacks imagined that to achieve black progress, the more privileged classes of blacks would have to become purveyors of civilization and uplift to the black masses. According to Gaines, while black elites hoped that the promotion of self-help through teachers, missionaries, and soldiers would challenge racial discrimination, the term "self-help" came to "signify the mere existence and stabilizing function of a 'civilized' black elite that had internalized the instrumental function of social control assigned to it." The promotion of racial uplift often framed black class stratification as evidence of progress. Thus, while the insistence on a "better class of blacks" challenged racial stereotypes, it also promoted them by characterizing the masses as degenerates whose salvation depended on the more privileged.[21]

Within this framework, black teachers served as an integral part of the class system that self-help ideology relied on. It is no surprise that the encounter between black teachers and the working classes was not entirely without class tensions. As early as the Reconstruction period, though the initial black teaching workforce included former slaves, many African-American teachers were descendants of free blacks.[22] In addition, many members of exclusive, affluent, mixed-race communities made up a portion of the teachers.[23] While this distinction suggests the unity between the free and freed, it is also indicative of growing class distinctions between blacks.

Though early self-uplift movements had encouraged the formulation of a racially unified community that included freed people, affluent free blacks, and those who had formerly been members of a separate caste, such as mixed-race communities in port cities, class stratification among blacks increased and condescension toward freed people was not unheard of. In fact, a number of long-established free black communities refused to educate their children alongside the children of the newly freed.[24] While many affluent blacks and mixed-race people rushed to the aid of freed people to act as educators and political leaders, historical analyses of the relationship between many mixed-race leaders and blacks during Reconstruction reveal the paternalism of this arrangement and sometimes endorse it. Joel Williamson has described the alliance thus: "Faced with an outrightly hostile white population, North and South, and a grudging, parsimonious government, black people needed the help that sophisticated, resourceful, and aggressive mulattos could give them."[25] Thus, implicit in the act of assuming the responsibility of meeting the needs of the black community was the presumption of superiority that discredited the ability of freed people to govern themselves.

Both Harper and Chesnutt had first-hand knowledge of the expectations for black teachers as community leaders and the complex class distinctions that sometimes separated black teachers from their students. In 1850, Harper began her career as a teacher at the Union Seminary, an African Methodist Episcopal school in Ohio, where she was the first female teacher at the Union Seminary.[26] She also delivered numerous lectures and published essays on the importance of education and helped establish educational programs. Chesnutt taught in rural schools outside of Charlotte, North Carolina, and by the age of 22 became the principal of the Fayetteville Normal School in 1880.[27] In fact, according to Charles Hackenberry, Chesnutt drew on his journals from his 1875 teaching stint at the Macedonia school near Spartanburg, South Carolina, in developing *Mandy Oxendine.*[28] The experiences of Harper and Chesnutt as teachers also confronted them with the cultural differences that class interjected into the black schoolroom. Both writers were well aware of the class differences between themselves and their students, and both felt somewhat alienated from their students. Harper was troubled by her inability to motivate her students in Little York, Pennsylvania, in 1852. Though Harper's education ended at the age of 13 when she left school to work as a domestic, her early schooling had afforded her exceptional academic preparation that her own pupils most likely would not have had. As Frances Smith Foster has noted, Harper's training in classics, elocution, and biblical studies at the William Watkins Academy, an elite school located in Baltimore founded by Harper's uncle may not have equipped her to teach a group that William Still has described as "fifty-three untrained little urchins."[29] Similarly, despite his position within the community as principal of the school, Chesnutt described himself as living "in a place whose people do not enter into my train of thoughts and who indeed cannot understand or sympathize with them."[30] Both Chesnutt and Harper contended with a sense of estrangement that complicated their teaching experiences.

The Merging of Figures: Mixed-Race Characters as Teachers

This historical framework illuminates the social and political implications of portrayals of black teachers in the literature of the era. If teachers represented who black people should be, then to discuss the roles of black teachers was to debate the future course of African Americans. If teachers were political leaders, then the portrayal of black teachers would engage the black political economy. And if teaching was a site of class tensions between middle-class and working-class blacks, then portrayals of black teachers would illustrate the clash of values, commitments, objectives, and cultures that stratified black communities. Near-white figures become agents to dramatize cultural conflict between black middle-class leaders and the black masses. By portraying schoolteachers as mulatto figures who by their resemblance to whites represent the potential to abandon black social causes, Harper and Chesnutt reflect on the supposed duties of the black middle class in determining the political and social direction of African-American communities.

Harper uses Iola Leroy's role as a schoolteacher to facilitate her assumption of the role of black leader, demonstrating the intimate ties between schoolteaching and community activism. As Carla Peterson has pointed out, *Iola Leroy* offers a "narrative of African-American institutional history, particularly that of church and school."[31] Iola's experience reflects that of many African-American teachers during Reconstruction. She establishes a school in the basement of a black church, and young and old travel from distant communities to learn. She soon finds that she must turn some away because of overcrowding. Iola vows to offer her students not only liberal education but also character training to make them good citizens. The narrator intimates how this kind of training could shape the values of black communities by infiltrating the home: "The school was beginning to lift up the home, for Iola was not satisfied to teach her children only the rudiments of knowledge. She had tried to lay the foundation of good character."[32] Though the text never refers to Iola as a teacher of industrial skills, she does not object to industrial education and endorses a combination of liberal and practical education.

Harper emphasizes Iola's role as a community leader by describing her efforts toward the improvement of the community more than she narrates her work in the classroom. At a salon in which various leaders address black community issues, Iola is invited to speak, and she takes "The Education of Mothers" as her topic. Throughout the novel, Iola insists on the importance of women's education. She counsels mothers, offers guidance for young girls, and delivers speeches to men and women about the future of the race. Iola later retires from her career as public schoolteacher and marries another educated nearly white mulatto who shares her dedication to racial uplift. She resumes her teaching career as a Sunday school teacher, emphasizing the important role of the Sabbath school tradition in an age of increasing child labor.

Harper's positioning of Iola as a schoolteacher and race reformer is problematic; Iola's only prior relation to blacks was as their mistress. When she considers the prospect of a teaching career while working as a Union nurse during the Civil War, she boasts that she was a favorite of the slave children on her father's plantation, demonstrating the only scheme in which she can configure her relation to black people. The dialect of many of the black characters is quaint to Iola, but it is familiar to her through memories of her plantation mammy. Indeed, her limited interaction with freedpeople seems to make her ill-fitted to assume the role of community leader. But as Hazel Carby has noted, in the context of Harper's novel, Iola's Western education and her middle-class values allow her to be a schoolteacher.[33] Her education and the class identification that it signifies become her passport to her role as a community leader. Though other critics have argued that Harper does not discredit the value of rural black culture, the promotion of Western cultural superiority in the text is difficult to refute.[34] For example, what makes Iola a teacher for mothers when she has no children herself? And why is it assumed that former slave women who had cared for white children for generations would not know how to parent?

Harper's use of a middle-class mixed-race character in the role of community leader has incited much controversy. Critics have been unforgiving of the seeming incongruity between the text's attention to the problems of the black masses and its reliance on a nearly white character as an example of black self-uplift. Barbara Christian has argued that *Iola Leroy* describes "a black middle class headed by mulattos who feel a grave responsibility of defining for the black race what is best for it."[35] Vashti Lewis adds that Harper is "guilty albeit unwittingly of the perpetuation of an image of black women in this country that suggests that those who have dark skin and whose hair is not straight are not only ugly but also never experience tragedy in their lives."[36] Others, including Deborah McDowell, have argued that Harper used nearly white characters to pander to a white audience.[37]

On the contrary, I argue that Harper's choice of a mixed-race figure as a heroine places the novel in conversation with other interracial fictions. Mixed-race characters perform as cultural signifiers that communicate the ways in which racial categorization was central to American nationhood in the United States. As in Harper's earlier novel *Minnie's Sacrifice,* in *Iola Leroy* the heroine's transformation from white to black is paralleled with the nation's transition from slave to free as the Civil War takes place. Iola, like Minnie, operates as a representative figure who illustrates the negotiation of national identity. But unlike mulatto fiction that evokes a mulatto-in-Eden configuration, Harper situates Iola's Edenic period in the novel's past. Using flashbacks, Harper examines Iola's life as a privileged young white woman before the war through the lens of her subsequent enslavement and her life as a freed slave after the war. Eden is always an illusion, a murky past so illusory that Iola refers to it as a "dream."[38] Indeed, Iola's support of the institution of slavery before she discovers that she too is a slave demonstrates how the myth of an American Eden was the invention of the white dreamer, never the black slave.

Harper's merging of the mixed-race figure with the figure of the teacher serves two functions. First, Harper transfers the focus of mixed-race fiction from the failure of white people to uphold the dream of democracy to the efforts of black people to challenge the prevailing racial thought and reshape definitions of nation and citizenship. Second, Harper dramatizes the conflict between personal advancement and collective interests through the choices the mulatto figure makes to be white or black, to abandon black social causes or to use her advantages to benefit the black community. The wide disparity between Iola's racial and class status and that of the black masses illustrates the growing class tensions within black communities. By framing her mulatto character as a teacher, someone who supposedly reflects a model for unified African-American progress as one who has also occupied the extremes of social strata, Harper attempts to diminish this friction. Iola's life journey has taken her from black to white, from slave to free, from rich to poor, and it integrates the experiences of the exceedingly privileged as well as the severely degraded to demonstrate the necessity of a unified effort toward black advancement.

Mixed-Race Figures and Individualism

Chestnutt's depiction of a mixed-race schoolteacher suggests that the options for the black self—subjugation by whites or communal activism on behalf of blacks—are narrow possibilities that inhibit the individual. The protagonist's resistance to becoming either a racial leader or a symbol of racial oppression poses challenges to the narrow ideologies of race and emphasizes the importance of the individual regardless of racial classification. This is not to suggest that Lowry's life is not shaped by the fiction of race but rather that Chesnutt employs a mixed-race figure, one whose racial category is unreadable, to consider the self-actualization of the individual beyond the narrow confines of racial classification. The schoolteacher who is considered black and yet can pass as white becomes a figure through which Chesnutt explores the plight of the individual in face of communal expectations and racial exclusion.

Chesnutt explores how a complex web of differences between the individual and the community shapes the mulatto schoolteacher's choices. The very differences that make Iola capable of becoming a dedicated community leader make Lowry ill-suited as a representative for rural blacks. By illustrating how class, color, and educational boundaries merge to form a cultural breach that separates the teacher and the town, Chesnutt challenges the responsibility of black middle-class teachers for the working-class black majority; indeed, he questions their adequacy for this task. Chesnutt offers a teacher who is neither a devoted community activist nor a white-identified person alienated from the black community. Lowry is an accepted member of a black community and is dispassionate about that community's interests. His self-absorbed posture is best captured in the novel's central narrative; he obtains a teaching job at the Sandy Run Colored School not for the sake of racial uplift but rather in pursuit of his childhood sweetheart, the nearly white title character, Mandy Oxendine. When he learns that she has relocated to this rural town in North Carolina, Lowry plans to follow her and arranges to take a position as a teacher to support himself while there. When he arrives, he discovers to his dismay that Mandy is living as white; his position as the colored teacher makes it difficult for him to have any contact with her. In addition, Mandy is being pursued by a white aristocrat, Utley, whom she is determined to marry, though she wants to keep Lowry as a second choice. When Utley is killed in an attempt to rape Mandy, the novel becomes a murder mystery. Mandy is arrested, and to save her, Lowry confesses to the crime. Within hours, the teacher has a lynching rope around his neck. Finally, in a rapid succession of events, they are both rescued and they run away together, though the narrator tells us it is unknown whether they live as black or white in their new life.

Chesnutt's representation of Lowry's complex views on race as shaped by his own family history indicates the singularity of his position. Lowry has grown up among blacks and other mixed-race people, and though he feels no intense commitment to the uplift of blacks, he has no real inclination to permanently pass as white either, though he passes occasionally. But Lowry's reason for declining to pass conflicts with Iola's self-sacrificial convictions. He chooses not to pass permanently because he believes that to do so would suggest that he is ashamed of slave ancestry, and he proudly maintains that he has no such ancestry. As the narrator puts it,

> [Lowry] was not responsible for his drop of dark blood. He had come by it honestly, for his father and mother, who were both of his own class, had been lawfully wedded. He had never been a slave, nor so far as tradition told of his ancestry, had he ever had a slave ancestor.[39]

Chesnutt's uncoupling of "black" and "slave" challenges assumptions of a racial commonality. Lowry's association of shame with the slave past is a striking departure from Iola's mission to reclaim that past and repair the family ties it had severed. His pride in his remoteness from slavery points to his acute resentment of the conflation of race and class. But unlike Iola, who attempts to extend her middle-class values to the masses, Lowry's desire to achieve personal class mobility unrestricted by racial identity shapes the core of his character, particularly his intense ambition. He dreams of fame, though the narrator never divulges in what capacity he hopes to achieve recognition. But Lowry also discerns that whiteness alone does not ensure class status. As an aspiring young man, he concludes that if he does accomplish anything great, people will discover his origins, and if he does not do something great, then it will be "merely a choice of mud-puddles, whether he should be a white tadpole or a black one."[40] Lowry's choice not to pass is influenced by his recognition that to be poor and white is little better than to be black. This awareness of the complicated intersections of racial and class boundaries displaces the relinquishing of whiteness as the ultimate sacrifice.

Also in contrast to Iola, whose education allows her to assume the role of schoolteacher and community leader, Lowry's education sparks his preference for personal advancement over community progress. As he pursues higher education, Lowry reads of great nations that had expired, civilizations that had decayed, philosophies and religious systems that had faded, and he concludes that there was "little an individual could accomplish compared with the achievements of the [human] race."[41] It is an irony that Lowry's education is the product of freedmen's school initiatives and white northern philanthropy in support of black colleges. Instead of making Lowry a community leader, his education inspires class aspirations that revolve around a desire for wealth and opportunity. This narrative revision foregrounds the economics of Iola's and Lowry's social positions. As a person who has lived most of her life as a wealthy white woman, Iola has privileges to renounce, thus allowing her to perform acts of self-sacrifice. In contrast, segregation and meager resources have shaped Lowry's life, and he uses this one kernel of philanthropic benevolence to gain a foothold on financial independence and social mobility. For Lowry, immediate practical issues, such as subsistence, are crucial. Lowry's interpretation of his liberal education in support of personal motives illustrates the privilege embedded in the communal perspective that Iola adopts.

Lovers and Leaders

Through Lowry's relationship with Mandy, Chesnutt elucidates the teacher's preoccupation with personal achievement and his growing indifference toward the black community. In contrast to Harper's neat pairing of two mulatto figures drawn to each other through their commitment to racial advancement, Chesnutt offers a pair united by the pursuit of social mobility. Like Lowry, Mandy seeks social advancement but believes her best opportunity to be marriage to an aristocrat. Such a marriage would require her to pass as white, but passing poses no moral dilemma for Mandy, who despises visibly black people, whom she refers to as "black, an' ugly an' pore."[42] Though Lowry gently scolds Mandy for such statements, he is so engrossed in his pursuit of her that her opinions matter little to him, and he even consents to pass as white when Mandy makes it clear that he must do so in order to be with her. Consumed with reuniting with Mandy, Lowry becomes neglectful of his primary duties as an instructor. The children become like shadows to him as he daydreams of Mandy. He dismisses school early to intercept her, and he even plots to escape lingering students after school to enable his secret interludes with her.

Despite the teacher's apathy toward black community interests and his avid self-involvement, Chesnutt frames him within circumstances that figure him as an involuntary racial leader, parodying the coalescence of the teacher and racial activist roles. The whites immediately resent Lowry because they are bitter about the expense that black public education is costing their community, which is still recovering from the economic losses of the war. In addition, by offering the children an education, Lowry is disrupting the child labor force and probably lessening the probability that the children will become adult wage laborers; their education, in theory, is preparing them for other work. While the political implications of Lowry's job figure him as a community leader, Lowry never consciously imagines himself as having any community responsibility. Nonetheless, the black community's response to Lowry demonstrates their high regard for him as a distinguished addition to their community and a potential leader. Though they sense a difference in color and culture between him and themselves and are "shy . . . of this white young man, who looked and bore himself so little like one of themselves," they immediately ask him to take a Sunday school class, demonstrating their confidence in his commitment to the community beyond his employment in the classroom.[43] They welcome him with much ceremony and overwhelm him with their attempts to socialize with him. The town's most distinguished black citizen, Mr. Revels, offers one of his daughters and a dowry of land to him.

By portraying Lowry as maintaining a state of detached amusement in his contact with rural blacks, notwithstanding their esteem for him, Chesnutt delineates the ideological gulf that divides the teacher from the folk community. Reflecting Lowry's consciousness, the narrator at times mocks everything from the polite conversation of rural blacks to their cultural values, and ultimately the everyday conduct of rural blacks is crude and immature to Lowry. For example, when he arrives, his host Deacon Pate quickly delivers a speech on the purposes of education:

> [L]arnin, aftah all, is jes' sump'n ter git sump'n e'se wid—kin' of a hook ter go fishin' wid. It'll he'p you to read de Bible and to understan' religion mo' an' better, an' it'll he'p you 'arn money fer ter buy chickens wid. Fer de ole style er gittin' chickens is mos' played out in dese days.[44]

Though Lowry finds Pate "witty" and sometimes even "shrewd," he also thinks he is "by no means profound enough to be worthy of record."[45] Pate's speech suggests a surreptitious jibe at Chesnutt's longtime friend Booker T. Washington.[46] Despite their friendship, Chesnutt was somewhat ambivalent about Washington's support of industrial education for blacks. In the context of a novel that portrays a reluctant black educator and leader, this somewhat disparaging allusion to Washington challenges the notion of representative race leaders, especially those whose elevated positions were heavily influenced by whites. As the scene unfolds, Pate's attempt to initiate a dialogue deteriorates into unilateral expression and indifferent silence, demonstrating the fallacy that black thought is monolithic. Through Lowry's assumed role of dispassionate observer, Chesnutt illustrates that there is no potential for an exchange of ideas between the men, confirming the depth of the cultural chasm between them.

This representation of uneducated blacks is distinct from Harper's. Though Harper represents the folk as in need of the services of a schoolteacher capable of instructing the masses about the duties and rights of citizenship and moral character, she also demonstrates their capacity for learning if given the chance. As Mary Elkins has noted, Harper's opening scene, which reveals the secret code used by the black community to communicate news of the war, discloses Harper's more complicated portrayal of the folk.[47] By discussing the condition of eggs and fish, they convey whether the North or the South is winning the war. Harper portrays the folk as capable of shrewdness and an abstract understanding of the world. In contrast, Pate's inability to understand the world beyond its practical value distinguishes him as forever exiled from the intellectual space that Lowry occupies. Though Lowry hopes to receive practical rewards for his talents, he also eagerly experiences the "intoxication of learning," and Pate's empirical evaluation of education demonstrates the obstacles between two men.[48] Lowry's resistance to the traditional role of African-American teachers challenges the paternal implications of that role. Despite Lowry's indifference, he does not pity the folk or assume the responsibility of uplifting them. He accepts the distance between himself and the folk without interpreting it as their inability to take responsibility for themselves. In this sense, Chesnutt presents an alternative to the prevailing doctrine that the future of black people would rely on middle-class blacks lending help to the working classes.

Nonetheless, Chesnutt compounds the sense of alienation between Lowry and the folk through his portrayal of Lowry's teaching experiences. His encounters with the children he teaches demonstrate the complicated social divisions that limit his potential to be a racial leader. Rather than offering speeches on moral development, Lowry responds to the children's morally questionable views with amusement and feigned agreement. His acquaintance with a particular student, Rose Amelia Sunday, captures the sense of detachment and condescension that defines his relationship with the children. A passionate child, Rose Amelia is romantically fixated on Lowry, who is unaware of her obsession and has no idea that Rose Amelia follows him around regularly. Indeed, Lowry's consistent inability to recognize Rose Amelia's presence becomes the definitive representation of his impotence as a communal leader. Frequently, Lowry literally cannot see Rose Amelia though she is standing near him. When he does occasionally notice her, he sees her as an entertaining environmental detail. He is amused by her appearance, which strikes him as a "contrast between the old and wizened look of her ugly little face . . . and the meager childish figure surmounted by it."[49] He is unable to determine her age, an example of the ways he is unable to read or understand her. His abbreviated understanding of her is evident when she recites her name, "Mississippi Nova Scotia Rose Amelia Sunday," and he immediately shortens it in the school ledger without considering her preference.[50]

Chesnutt's treatment of Rose Amelia and the burden of her black body also indicate how Lowry's fair skin contributes to his disassociation. Chesnutt shifts the role traditionally associated with the mixed-race character by characterizing Rose Amelia, the dark-skinned black character, as the one who is trapped in a body that doesn't fit her inner identity and who dies wretchedly as a result. Chesnutt portrays her as inhabiting a body that does not allow her to realize her aristocratic principles and bars her from fulfilling her hopeless love for Lowry: "Rose Amelia's soul was that of an aristocrat, which by some wanton freak of fate had been locked up in a chrysalis from which it could never emerge."[51] When she realizes that her attempt to have Mandy imprisoned to save Lowry from being accused of Utley's murder has forced Lowry to confess to the crime to save Mandy, Rose Amelia is emotionally shattered. She is found dead the following day, and the narrator ambiguously implies that she committed suicide to atone for her act, which she believed would lead to Lowry's death. This narratological dislocation underscores color as a determinant of Lowry's role as a detached witness within the Sandy Run community. By substituting the black body for the mulatto body as the site of a conflicted identity that initiates an ill-fated sequence of events, Chesnutt foregrounds the different degrees of social mobility that the bodies of Mandy and Lowry facilitate.

Lowry's identification of himself as black in the town of Sandy Run becomes a powerful determinant of his social role. Just as class divides Lowry from this black community, his assigned racial identity makes him victim to the white community. In Chesnutt's novel, the critical juncture is not the internal choice to become a teacher and social activist but rather the externally imposed exposure to the lynching block, where the choice to live or die is not Lowry's own. Despite his disinterest in black communal causes, he is reduced to a symbol of racial injustice and violence. In the depiction of Lowry's near-lynching, the narrator calls attention to the national implications of the lynching crisis in the 1890s: "The lynching fever which has since swept over the South and disgraced the nation, had at that time not yet broken out, but the memory of the Ku Klux Klan was still green, and elsewhere in the South there were plenty of precedents both for the act and for a probable immunity from punishment."[52] Chesnutt's darkly comic representation of the lynch mob, however, suggests that the national crisis was being perpetrated by a group of buffoons. The mob is marked by divisions between some who are crudely bloodthirsty and those who seek to maintain the ritualistic nature of lynching, though they are unclear about exactly what the ritual should include. Lowry's quiet dignity in the face of their raucous confusion and the relative absence of dialect in his speech, which is juxtaposed with their pronounced dialect, indicates his superior education, intellect, and class status. Even though he is better educated and far more intelligent than his persecutors, Lowry lives at their will. Though a white minister in the town confesses to the crime for which Lowry is to be lynched, members of the mob consider lynching Lowry anyway for having said that he killed a white man. When someone proposes that they lynch the minister instead, the mob concludes that to lynch a white man would compromise the principles of American justice: "[T]he right to trial by jury is one o' the bull-works of our libbutty."[53] Thus, Lowry is reduced to an emblem of national injustice. His rapid trajectory from schoolroom to lynching block suggests that confronting racial discrimination is not restricted to those who resolve to sacrifice their lives for racial advancement. In light of Harper's text and the general call for racial advancement through teachers and other racial leaders, this portrayal also suggests that personal experience with racism was trial enough without assuming responsibility for all black people. Still, Lowry escapes lynching, and he and Mandy go away together. The ambiguity about which race they choose in their new life is Chesnutt's final displacement of racial identification as the definitive determinant of the individual.

Class, Education, and Opportunity

Chesnutt imagines class differences as gaping cultural rifts between the mixed-race schoolteacher and the town; Harper envisions them as ripe opportunities for improving the masses. Though it would be reductive to read Harper's and Chesnutt's literary contributions as mere extensions of their educational values, their works reflect their discordant experiences and offer insight into how they construct and justify the social choices their protagonists make. Lowry's sense of difference between himself and a community located only miles from where he grew up is better understood in light of the difference between Chesnutt's education and that of the nearby rural blacks he would later teach. Similarly, Iola's sense of duty expressed in her choice to become a teacher and leader among a community that she knows little about is illuminated by Harper's immersion in the common political interests of slaves and free blacks during the antebellum era. Harper's essays and Chesnutt's journals offer reflections of how each writer's experiences as both teachers and students informed their representation of the self-help movement and the role of schoolteachers within it.

Harper's theory of the role of teachers in self-help movements is best expressed in her 1885 essay "A Factor in Human Progress," in which she describes a black schoolteacher in the South who complains of a "lack of society" among a gossiping black community. Harper explains that instead of complaining about her neighbors and shunning them, the schoolteacher should be educating them in conversation, parenting, and temperance. Harper offers this monologue that describes what such a woman should resolve to do when faced with gossiping neighbors:

> These women cannot improve me, but I will try to improve them. If they talk nothing but gossip, I will try to raise the tone of conversation. . . . I will study to teach these mothers how to take care of their little ones; I will learn something of the sophistries of strong drink, . . . and teach them how intemperance adds to the burdens, waste and miseries of society, because I have had advantages that were denied them; as a friend and sister, I will gladly share with them my richer heritage . . . for the best test of an education is not simply what we know, but what we do, and what we are.[54]

Harper suggests that rather than lamenting cultural differences, the teacher might narrow those differences through instruction and by example. This educational model reflects the intimate ties between education and action and the notion of educational leadership as a propelling force for the cycle of uplift. Though Harper clearly outlines the leadership role that the teacher should assume beyond the classroom, her suggestion that she should study to learn about that community's needs demonstrates that Harper does not assume that her education equips her with an understanding of the needs of this particular community. Education is a tool that would allow her to seek out resources to learn about her community and apply that knowledge. Though Harper's relegation of intemperance and parental negligence to this community alone is reductive, her rebuke also implies the hypocrisy of a schoolteacher gossiping about the community's tendency to gossip. Thus, her criticism of this schoolteacher is also a critique of education for the purpose of pedantry.

Chesnutt's journals demonstrate a focus on the importance of education in combating ignorance, but they also reveal an almost hostile attitude toward the uneducated black masses:

> Well! Uneducated people are the most bigoted, superstitious, hardest headed people in the world! Those folks down stairs believe in ghost, luck, horse shoes . . . and all other kinds of nonsense, and all the argument in the world couldn't get it out of them. It is useless to argue with such persons. All the eloquence of a Demosthenes, the logic of Plato, the demonstrations of the most learned men in this world couldn't convince them of the falsity, the absurdity, the utter impossibility and unreasonableness of such things. Verily, education is a great thing, and I would I could quote a quire or two of Mayhew's Universal Education on the subject, "Education lessens and dissipates the effects of ignorance."[55]

While Chesnutt professes the importance of education, the sense of impenetrable class differences emerges as he points out that certain people are uneducable. Though it may seem odd that Chesnutt, a product of southern free schools, would have such impressions of rural blacks, his own educational opportunities bore little resemblance to theirs. As Richard Brodhead notes, Chesnutt's access to the Howard School of Fayetteville, North Carolina, a well-funded school initiated by blacks and the Freedmen's Bureau and funded by northern philanthropic support, offered him educational advantages that unsupported rural schools lacked the resources to provide. According to Brodhead, these educational advances that Chesnutt and others who attended well-funded schools enjoyed led to a growing diversified class structure with an emerging black intelligentsia at its helm. He points out that "doctors, lawyers, preachers, and especially educators—were taught in the new schools that arose with the end of slavery, and so were enabled by an education like Chesnutt's."[56] Although this education permitted many to become leaders in the effort to lift the black masses, it also produced a changing sense of social identity that made them "experience themselves as different *from* the masses."[57] This feeling of difference that is so evident in Chestnut's journals elucidates the impression of cultural difference that Lowry experiences in his social transactions with the folk characters.

Some of the differences in how each author approaches the role of schoolteachers and issues of class within self-help movements stem from chronological differences of the pre–Civil War era in which Harper grew up and the Reconstruction era in which Chesnutt came of age. While Chesnutt was receiving the educational advantages that Reconstruction allowed, Harper was already educating as she traveled the South as a full-time lecturer. Though like Chesnutt, Harper had the advantages of a better education than many of her peers, she had also experienced the precarious situation of so-called free blacks in the North during the antebellum years.[58]

When she came to adulthood in the midst of the controversy over the Compromise of 1850, Harper was living in Maryland as a free black in a slave state at a time when the lines between slave and free could shift at any moment due to the Fugitive Slave Act. Not long after, Harper's family was forced by local officials to disband their elite school for blacks and sell their home. Unable to return to Maryland after 1853 because of a law forbidding free blacks to enter the state, Harper committed herself to the antislavery cause when a free black man was arrested and enslaved for entering Maryland.[59]

Harper's precarious existence as a free black person in the antebellum era undoubtedly shaped her sense of duty to the communal cause of African-American freedom. The dubious distinctions between slave and free meant that though there may have been class differences between the groups, their political interests were intimately connected as black and slave became increasingly interchangeable. Though Harper may have had educational advantages, the vulnerability of her own freedom was inextricably linked to slavery, and her emphasis on the importance of the community reflects the sense of collective duty and sacrifice that the antislavery cause necessitated. By beginning Iola's trajectory with slavery, Harper evokes this unifying African-American experience to elicit a call for African-American collective activism. Harper poses Iola's life as a microcosm of the collective history of African Americans as she passes through slavery, Reconstruction, and, often implicitly, Redemption. Harper's depiction of Iola's choice to become an African-American schoolteacher as one that was born from this historical experience poses Iola's sacrifice and community activism as an opportunity for all African Americans. Harper offers a narrative of African-American progress and the teacher-as-activist as the ultimate means of achieving that goal.

Harper's and Chesnutt's approaches to education also reflect the differences in opportunities available to men and women at the turn of the century. By embracing self-help ideology, Harper could create a space for a black woman to assume a position of leadership. The role of teacher mediates between gender spheres, encompassing both domestic and public roles. The political leadership embedded in the perception of the duties of black schoolteachers illuminates the wider political implications for black women who assumed this role. If schoolteachers could be considered representatives of the race, black women could represent themselves within the larger political context. While Harper's male characters contribute and become community leaders through various occupations, including doctors, soldiers, preachers, and teachers, her female characters, such as Iola, Lucy, Minnie of *Minnie's Sacrifice,* and Annette of *Trial and Triumph* have just one outlet—teaching. Iola's brother Harry becomes the head of the school along with his wife, Lucille, but Harry has also been an officer in a black Civil War regiment, demonstrating the multiple choices at his disposal. Harper emphasizes that Iola chooses teaching because of the social work that it involves, but she also demonstrates that the few other occupations open to Iola would not allow her to become a race leader to benefit the black community. While working at a store under a kind employer, Iola states: "I am preparing to teach, and must spend my leisure time in study. . . . [T]o be an expert accountant is not the best use to which I can put my life."[60] Thus, teaching becomes the primary way for women to contribute to the self-help movement and a way of promoting public roles for women as their duty rather than a mere possibility. This emphasis on communal duty also reflects a desire for political advancement for black women.

Though both writers employ mixed-race characters to explore the relationship between the black middle and working classes, the historical differences that emerge with the pairing of Chesnutt's and Harper's fiction illuminate how generational concerns influence their works. Indeed, envisioning Chesnutt's generation, one that grew up in the midst of increasing class differences, as a potential audience for Harper's novel solves the riddle of why she returned to a plot that she had already begun in her earlier novel *Minnie's Sacrifice* (1869), a narrative that is also driven by a mixed-race character whose acknowledgment of her slave past initiates her leadership in a black community. While she acknowledges the class differences of the postwar era, Harper injects the schoolteacher figure into mixed-race fiction, capitalizing on this symbol of the black middle class to demonstrate how class differences might be points of connection rather than barriers between groups. Juxtaposing Iola's ability to pass as white with her decision to use her skills to prepare blacks for citizenship, Harper employs the element of mixed race to dramatize what she saw as the choices available to the black middle class—abandonment of black social causes or commitment to them. In contrast, Chesnutt's representation of the mixed-race schoolteacher posits class as more than material differences that can be extended to others. Instead, he uses class as a powerful idea that shapes one's understanding of self and community. Chesnutt uses the mixed-race character, the self that cannot easily be read or categorized, to consider the dilemma of the individual in a nation whose sense of order depends on racial categories. The lines of race function as boundaries that shift at will in both novels, but the lines of class pose a more difficult terrain. In *Iola Leroy,* the barriers between teachers and their communities can be surpassed only through carefully built bridges of educational uplift, but in *Mandy Oxendine,* they function as one-way channels, across which schoolteachers such as Lowry can never return.

Epilogue: Formulating a National Self

It should not be surprising that mixed-race characters engaged the discourse of nation and citizenship in the United States. One need only consider how the U.S. census has grappled with the categorization of mixed-race peoples to recognize how race continues to be integral to defining national identities, histories, and social agendas. Indeed, the history of the attempts of the U.S. census to define and categorize race might be read as a narrative of national identity formation. As Clarence Lusane points out, racial categories have been defined differently in nearly every U.S. census. In 1790, the first U.S. census categories consisted of free white males, free white females, all other free persons (by sex and color), and slaves. The 1850 census added a special box for color and specified that enumerators were to leave the box blank for white persons, but they were to enter "B" for blacks and "M" for mulattos.[1] The instructions to enumerators demonstrate how whiteness was equated with citizenship; it needs no designation because it is what defines American. In contrast, black and mixed-race individuals required designation and explanation.

As Melissa Nobles points out, though the census has been presented as unbiased measurement, it participates in the construction of race as it relates to citizenship: "[C]ensuses help form racial discourse, which in turn affects the public policies that either vitiate or protect the rights, privileges, and experiences commonly associated with citizenship."[2] The addition of the designation for mixed-race people in the 1850 census expresses the ways in which the notion of mixed race presented problems for racial ideologies that supported white supremacy and segregation. Nobles argues that this sudden interest in recording biracial people was sparked by polygenesis theories that argued that people of different racial groups had separate biological origins. If black and white people had different origins, then mixing the two groups could not produce healthy populations. Theories that purported to explain the infertility or high mortality rates of mixed-race people were used to substantiate the theory of polygenesis, and they ultimately were used to argue for the necessity of segregation and antimiscegenation laws.[3] The administrators of the 1850 census constructed categories to provide evidence for the necessity of racial subjugation in order to ensure the legitimacy and even necessity of oppressive measures against people of African descent.[4] That census administrators attempted to document the decline of mixed-race people points to the threat that hybridity posed to popular racial ideologies.

In 1890, the beginning of a decade marked by escalating lynchings intended to punish real or imagined trespasses of the color line, census designations for people of African descent increased to include "quadroon," and "octoroon." Collectors were directed to "be particularly careful to distinguish between blacks, mulattos, quadroons, and octoroons."[5] The expansion of these categories expresses the national anxiety about the unintelligibility of race. This series of categories and the unending possibilities of additional categories that loom at its edges convey the desire to name the not-American in order to define the American. The attempts of census recorders to locate and order blackness make apparent the dread of the unidentifiable other that can pass for white. The census of 1920 was the last to include categories for mixed-race people.

In 1930, census enumerators were instructed that anyone mixed with "Negro blood" should be counted as Negro, except in the case of a Negro-Indian mixture in which "Indian blood predominates and the status of an Indian is generally accepted in the community."[6] Hence, the census adopted what is commonly known as "the one-drop rule." These guidelines signify the desire to designate blackness, visible or invisible, as the most important racial category to mark individuals as different from both the white population and other nonwhite populations. In addition, the instructions concerning individuals of black and Native American backgrounds implies both the readability of race and an intriguing disregard for the crossing of boundaries between these two severely oppressed groups. But blackness remains an unforgivable stain on both the national conscious and the national body.

If the direction of each census tells us something about the conceptual relationship between race and nation at any given time, we might ask what the 2000 census tells us about current racial ideologies. It was the first census in U.S. history in which respondents were allowed to identify more than one racial category to which they belonged. Various civil rights groups opposed this measure, arguing that because so many African Americans could cite evidence of racial mixture, choosing multiple categories would severely decrease African-American numbers and thus impact social policy decisions. Nonetheless, 34 million people identified themselves by African American only, while just over 6 million people identified themselves with two or more races. Despite all the controversy and the billions of dollars spent to conduct and process the census, the U.S. Office of Management and Budget determined that in order to monitor and enforce civil rights, federal agencies would assign responses that combined the racial category white and one minority group to the minority group. The purpose of this allocation was to protect the civil rights of historically oppressed groups; in its attempt to regulate the treatment of these groups, the rule outlines the workings of contemporary racial ideology. It presumes that a cultural tendency to classify mixed-race peoples according to their nonwhite family history is the most likely cause of racial discrimination. This tabulation of race operates as a one-drop rule, even as it attempts to regulate this rule. It demonstrates that hybridity itself must be reduced to something readable in the context of the popular understanding of race.

While my own book concerns mixed-race characters, not mixed-race people, I cite this troubled relationship between citizen and census to demonstrate how race has been and continues to be integral to the formulation of a national self. Though many writers of interracial fiction have been dismissed as sensationalistic, misguided, and, in the case of black writers, self-hating, I argue that these writers recognized that including mixed-race characters placed a particular set of issues on the table, more specifically the discourse of race and nation. This is certainly not to suggest that these writers necessarily agreed on what that relationship means or how it should be enforced or redressed but rather that mixed-race characters were the vehicle through which to enter the conversation. The conflict between the white skins of mixed-race characters and their imputed blackness served to racialize whiteness, to both name it and express the impossibility of naming it by relying on what it is not. Mixed-race characters could express the readable boundary between the races as well as the crossing of that boundary. They could be used to construct race, to define it by tracing its margins, but they could also dismantle it by illustrating the dissolution of binaries. The importance of mulatto figures in American literature is the way in which they reflect and deflect the invention of race.

I began this book by focusing on a scene in *Iola Leroy* in which a mixed-race character refuses a marriage proposal from a white lover because this moment reflects so much of what mixed-race literature has been criticized for. The scene is rife with the trappings of melodrama: an ardent, hopeful lover and a desperate girl, torn between her attraction to him and her duty to her family and her community. As if that were not enough, the lynchpin that informs the situational conflict is race, the invisible imp that stands between the lovers. But Harper could have produced melodrama without this final blow. The "barriers" that stand between Iola and her white lover become the main characters in this scene, naming the social, civic, and historical boundaries that defined the nation. Iola's refusal of the marriage proposal communicates the construction of racial categories, and yet her nearly white appearance introduces the figure of choice, indicating the permeability of these categories. That Iola chooses to live as black and dedicate her life to preparing blacks for the duties of American citizenship draws a connection between the boundaries between the lovers and those that shape the nation. The melodrama reflects the national melodrama that continues to grip Americans to this day.

The contemporary relevance of these issues suggests that this study might have gone on to consider the development of interracial fictions in the twentieth century as well. But with the advent of various modernisms, representations of racial mixing are complicated by the interiority of selfhood. Though these twentieth-century works certainly refer to the impact of social formations, the selves they present are more fragmented than national. Indeed, in twentieth-century American fiction, the genre of science fiction offers the most intriguing parallel to nineteenth-century interracial fiction. In *Dawn* (1987), Octavia Butler, like many writers of melodramatic mixed-race fiction, focuses on the figure of hybridity to produce a critique of social formations within a generic framework that is often dismissed as socially irrelevant. The central character, Lilith Iyapo, is coopted by the Oankali, alien beings who depend on exchanging genes with other beings for survival. At this point, a genetic flaw of human beings, their combination of intelligence with hierarchical inclinations, has led to the nuclear destruction of the world. Lilith is chosen as a mate for the Oankali and as a trainer for the remaining human beings who must also accept Oankali mates. Genetically altered by the Oankali to be stronger and smarter than other humans, Lilith is neither human nor Oankali. Lilith, as Michele Osherow notes, becomes a sort of Eve, ensuring the reproduction of both the Oankali and the humans, who are no longer allowed by the Oankali to reproduce on their own.[7] Just as nineteenth-century writers of interracial fictions evoked the myth of America as Eden to critique the state of the nation, Butler's Eve/Lilith suggests new beginnings that compel comparison to social conditions. While the Oankali-human contact evokes colonization, Butler complicates this binary of colonizer and colonized through her representation of Lilith's difficult negotiation between worlds. This negotiation is replete with contradictions that blur the distinctions between hierarchy and equality, love and exploitation, theft and exchange, commitment and betrayal. Butler's representation of Lilith as the hybrid figure compels us to consider the nature of social construction as well as the power of social categories and the agendas that they serve. Butler situates an old conflict in a new context. The building of a nation becomes the building of a world. But the binaries that she destabilizes through the intermixing of beings and cultures are familiar poles that nineteenth-century writers of mixed-race fiction also encountered.

When I began this project, I was overwhelmed by the copiousness of mixed-race fictions produced in the nineteenth century. Any comprehensive reading of mixed-race fiction might well have produced a multivolume work. This book, instead, offers one way of reading these texts in the context of national construction. To me, the abundance of these fictions suggests a relatively new nation seeking self-definition, naming and renaming itself into being. The stories of mixed-race fiction convey the larger narrative of competing attempts to tell the story of America, defining its goals, its failures, its changes, and its stasis. By dramatizing particular cultural conflicts and proposing solutions, these writers articulate and shape the national discourse. Just as they did in the nineteenth century, twentieth-century interracial fictions continue to offer a lens through which Americans might look at themselves.

Notes

Introduction

1. Frances E. W. Harper, *Iola Leroy, or Shadows Uplifted* (1892; reprint, New York: Mentor, 1992), 84.

2. Valerie Babb, *Whiteness Visible* (New York: New York University Press, 1998), 37.

3. Toni Morrison, *Playing in the Dark: Whiteness and the Literary Imagination* (New York: Random House, 1993), 52.

4. Sterling Brown outlines his theory of the "tragic mulatto" in *The Negro in American Fiction* (Washington, D.C.: The Association in Negro Folk Education, 1937), 43–44; he makes the point that the character was used mostly by white writers in the introduction to *The Negro Caravan,* ed. Sterling Brown, Arthur P. Davis, and Ulysses Lee (New York: Arno Press, 1970), 5–6.

5. For a thorough discussion of the "tragic mulatto" in literary criticism, see Werner Sollors, *Neither Black nor White yet Both: Thematic Explorations of Interracial Literature* (New York: Oxford University Press, 1997), 220–245.

6. Deborah McDowell, *"The Changing Same": Black Women's Literature Criticism, and Theory* (Bloomington: Indiana University Press, 1995), 39.

7. Houston A. Baker Jr., *Workings of the Spirit: The Poetics of Afro-American Women's Writing* (Chicago: University of Chicago Press, 1991), 25.

8. Ann Ducille, *The Coupling Convention: Sex, Text, and Tradition in Black Women's Fiction* (New York: Oxford University Press, 1993), 7.

9. Sollors, *Neither Black nor White yet Both,* 238.

10. Suzanne Bost, "Fluidity without Postmodernism: Michelle Cliff and the 'Tragic Mulatta' Tradition," *African American Review* 32, no. 4 (1998): 675; Ducille, *The Coupling Convention,* 24–25; Jean Fagan Yellin, *Women and Sisters: The Antislavery Feminists in American Culture* (New Haven: Yale University Press, 1989), 197–198.

11. Yellin, *Women and Sisters,* 53.

12. Jane Tompkins, *Sensational Designs* (New York: Oxford University Press, 1985), xvi.

13. Hazel Carby, *Reconstructing Womanhood: The Emergence of the Afro-American Woman Novelist* (New York: Oxford University Press, 1987), 89.

14. Tompkins, *Sensational Designs,* xvi.

15. According to Winthrop Jordan, many whites saw miscegenation as a sign that the American experiment had failed and that sin dominated in the New World. *White over Black: Attitudes Toward the Negro, 1550–1812* (Chapel Hill: University of North Carolina Press, 1968), 543.

16. R. W. B. Lewis, *The American Adam* (Chicago: University of Chicago Press, 1955), 5.

17. Sollors, *Neither Black nor White yet Both,* 241.

18. Morrison, *Playing in the Dark,* 45.

19. Ibid.

20. For a discussion of myths of racial signs, see Sollors, *Neither Black nor White yet Both,* 143–161.

21. Karen Sánchez-Eppler, *Touching Liberty: Abolition, Feminism, and the Politics of the Body* (Berkeley: University of California Press, 1993), 33.

21. Lauren Berlant, "National Brands/National Body: Imitation of Life," in *Comparative American Identities: Race, Sex, and Nationality in the Modern Text,* ed. Hortense J. Spillers (New York: Routledge, 1991), 113.

22. Ducille, *The Coupling Convention,* 9.

1. *The Last of the Mohicans* or the First of the Mulattos?

1. For a discussion of this revised masthead, see Mary Hershberger, "Mobilizing Women, Anticipating Abolition: The Struggle against Indian Removal in the 1830's," *Journal of American History* 86, no. 1 (1999): 36–37.

2. Hershberger, "Mobilizing Women, Anticipating Abolition," 17.

3. *The Liberator,* April 23, 1831.

4. Sterling Brown is credited with identifying Cora as the first mulatto figure in American literature. Sterling Brown, *The Negro in American Fiction* (Washington, D.C.: The Association of Negro Folk Education, 1937), 8.

5. Valerie Babb, *Whiteness Visible* (New York: New York University Press, 1998), 5.

6. David T. Haberly, "Women and Indians: *The Last of the Mohicans* and the Captivity Tradition," *American Quarterly* 28 (1976): 439; Jane Tompkins, *Sensational Designs* (New York: Oxford University Press, 1985), 106–109.

7. Leslie Fiedler, *Love and Death in the American Novel* (New York: Criterion, 1960), 203–205.

8. George Dekker and John P. McWilliams, *Fenimore Cooper: The Critical Heritage* (London: Routledge & Kegan Paul, 1973), 72.

9. Fiedler, *Love and Death in the American Novel,* 203–205.

10. James Madison, *Letters and Other Writings of James Madison* (Philadelphia: Lippincott & Co., 1865), 516. Madison made this statement in a February 10, 1826, letter to Thomas L. McKenny.

11. Richard Slotkin, *Regeneration through Violence: The Mythology of the American Frontier, 1600–1860* (New York: Harper Collins, 1996), 464.

12. Linda Kerber, "The Abolitionist Perception of the Indian," *Journal of American History* 62, no. 2 (1975): 271.

13. Herbert Aptheker, *Abolitionism: A Revolutionary Movement* (Boston: G. K. Hall & Co., 1989), 4–5.

14. Ibid., 13.

15. Ronald N. Satz, *American Indian Policy in the Jacksonian Era* (Lincoln: University of Nebraska Press, 1975), 1.

16. For discussions of Native American removal policy, see Richard Drinnon, *Facing West: The Metaphysics of Indian-Hating and Empire-Building* (Minneapolis: University of Minnesota Press, 1980); and Robert Berkhoffer, *The White Man's Indian: Images of the American Indian from Columbus to the Present* (New York: Knopf, 1978).

17. Quoted in Kerber, "The Abolitionist Perception of the Indian," 273.

18. Alexis de Tocqueville, *Democracy in America* (New York: Knopf, 1984), 332.

19. Kerber, "The Abolitionist Perception of the Indian," 273.

20. Hershberger, "Mobilizing Women, Anticipating Abolition," 22; Henry Mayer, *All On Fire: William Lloyd Garrison and the Abolition of Slavery* (New York: St. Martin's Press, 1998), 138.

21. Beriah Green, *Sketches of the Life and Writings of James Gillespie Birney* (Utica: Jackson and Chaplin, 1844), 7–8.

22. Hershberger, "Mobilizing Women, Anticipating Abolition," 22; Kerber, "The Abolitionist Perception of the Indian," 274–275.

23. Kerber, "The Abolitionist Perception of the Indian," 275.

24. P. J. Staudenraus, *The African Colonization Movement, 1816–1865* (New York: Columbia University Press, 1961), 104–116.

25. Ibid., 172.

26. Hershberger, "Mobilizing Women, Anticipating Abolition," 35.

27. William Lloyd Garrison, *Thoughts on African Colonization* (New York: Arno Press, 1969), part 2, 5.

28. Kenneth Wiggins Porter, "Negroes and the Seminole War, 1817–1818," *Journal of Negro History* 36, no. 3 (1951): 254.

29. J. Leitch Wright Jr., *Creeks & Seminoles: The Destruction of the Muscogulge People* (Lincoln: University of Nebraska Press, 1986), 190.

30. Carter G. Woodson, *The Negro in Our History* (Washington, D.C.: Associated Publishers, 1941), 193.

31. Kenneth Wiggins Porter, "Negroes and the Seminole Wars 1835–1842," *Journal of Negro History* 36, no. 3 (1951): 430.

32. Kerber, "The Abolitionist Perception of the Indian," 278.

33. *The Colored American,* March 27, April 3, and April 17, 1841.

34. Ibid., December 29, 1838.

35. Ibid., March 21, 1840. Nathaniel Southard was also the editor of the children's magazine *Youth Cabinet.*

36. *The Colored American,* April 17, 1841.

37. Cheryl Walker, *Indian Nation: Native American Literature and Nineteenth-Century Nationalisms* (Durham: Duke University Press, 1997), 3–11. As Walker notes, literary criticism has often overlooked the contributions of Native American literature to the discourse of American nationalism, assuming instead that Native Americans have generally been the victims of nationalist discourse. Walker offers a compelling argument for how Native American writers participated in conversations about American national identity.

38. Sharon Malinowski, Anna Sheets, and Linda Schmittroth, eds., *Encyclopedia of Native American Tribes* (Detroit: Gale Group, 1999), 1:154. Though the U.S. government did not admit Native Americans to full citizenship until 1924, the Brothertown Indians of Wisconsin petitioned for titles to individually held lands and requested U.S. citizenship in 1837 to prevent further westward removal. Congress granted the request in 1839, thus ending the federal government's responsibilities to the tribe. By becoming citizens, the Brothertown Indians of Wisconsin relinquished their status as a sovereign nation and lost recognition of their tribal government.

39. James Fenimore Cooper, *The Last of the Mohicans, a Narrative of 1757* (New York: Penguin, 1962), 188.

40. The plot in which Cooper develops Cora's ancestry is the same narrative that Lydia Maria Child would later use in her Reconstruction text *A Romance of the Republic* (1867), which sought to revive antislavery sentiment and transform it into support for integration. In Child's text, the irresponsible father who never frees the mother of his children leads to their enslavement. Through the narrative in which the father first chooses a white woman whom he is prevented from marrying and then begins a relationship with a woman of

African descent made available to him through slavery, Child deflects individual blame and focuses on reconciliation, positing the institution of slavery as the central villain.

41. Cooper, *The Last of the Mohicans,* 188.

42. Ibid., 187.

43. Fiedler, *Love and Death in the American Novel,* 204.

44. Toni Morrison, *Playing in the Dark: Whiteness and the Literary Imagination* (New York: Random House, 1993), 47.

45. R. W. B. Lewis, *The American Adam* (Chicago: University of Chicago Press, 1955), 5.

46. Donald Pease, *Visionary Compacts: American Renaissance Writings in Cultural Context* (Madison: University of Wisconsin Press, 1987), 20.

47. Winthrop Jordan, *White over Black: Attitudes Toward the Negro, 1550–1812* (Chapel Hill: University of North Carolina Press, 1968), 543. As Jordan points out, "a darkened nation would mean that animal sex governed American destiny and that the experiment in the wilderness had failed."

48. Lewis, *The American Adam,* 5.

49. Cooper, *The Last of the Mohicans,* 188.

50. James Fenimore Cooper, *The Travelling Bachelor; or, Notions of the Americans* (New York: Stinger and Townsend, 1852), 2:262–263.

51. Ibid., 2:263.

52. Ibid., 2:277.

53. Ibid., 2:282.

54. Ibid., 2:277.

55. Jordan, *White over Black,* 90.

56. Ibid., 91.

57. Slotkin, *Regeneration through Violence,* 21.

58. Robert Young, *Domesticating Slavery: The Master Class in Georgia and South Carolina, 1670–1837* (Chapel Hill: University of North Carolina Press, 1999), 185–186.

59. Cooper, *The Last of the Mohicans,* 162.

60. Williams Gilmore Simms, *The Yemassee: A Romance of Carolina,* ed. John Caldwell Guilds (Fayetteville: University of Arkansas Press, 1994), 397.

61. John Caldwell Guilds, "Introduction," in *The Yemassee: A Romance of Carolina* (Fayetteville: University of Arkansas Press, 1994), xx.

62. Tocqueville, *Democracy in America,* 332.

63. Ibid., 335–336.

64. Wright, *Creeks & Seminoles,* 232.

65. Cooper, *The Travelling Bachelor,* 2:278.

66. Thomas Jefferson, *Writings* (New York: Viking Press, 1984), 461–462.

67. Ibid., 266.

68. Young, *Domesticating Slavery,* 185.

69. Ibid., 211.

70. Cooper, *The Last of the Mohicans,* 356–357.

71. Ibid., 356–357.

72. Magdalene Mayer, "Racial Perceptions in James Fenimore Cooper's *The Last of the Mohicans,*" in *Blurred Boundaries: Critical Essays on American Literature,* ed. Klaus Schmidt and David Sawyer (Frankfurt: Peter Lang, 1996), 50.

73. Cooper, *The Last of the Mohicans,* 362.

74. Ibid., 374.

75. Ibid., 360.

76. Ibid., 360.
77. Drinnon, *Facing West,* 102.

2. A Land without Names

1. Lydia Maria Child, *The Liberator,* March 18, 1837, 47; reprinted in Patricia G. Holland, Milton Meltzer, and Francine Krasno, eds., *The Collected Correspondence of Lydia Maria Child, 1817–1880* (Millwood, N.Y.: Kraus Microform, 1980), fiche 67, letter 1789.
2. Richard Hildreth, introduction to *Archy Moore, the White Slave; or Memoirs of a Fugitive* (New York: Miller, Orton and Mulligan, 1856; reprint, New York: Negro Universities Press, 1969), ix.
3. John O. Sargent "The Slave or Memoirs of Archy Moore," *Boston Atlas,* December 24, 1836, 1. Like many, Sargent suspected that Lydia Maria Child was the author of the book.
4. Hildreth, introduction, xi–xii.
5. Evan Brandstater, "Uncle Tom and Archy Moore: The Antislavery Novel as Ideological Symbol," *American Quarterly* 26, no. 2 (1974): 160.
6. James Kinney, *Amalgamation! Race, Sex, and Rhetoric in the Nineteenth-Century American Novel* (Westport, Conn.: Greenwood Press, 1985), 47.
7. Brandstater, "Uncle Tom and Archy Moore," 168.
8. Jules Zanger, "The 'Tragic Octoroon' in Pre-Civil War Fiction," *American Quarterly* 18, no. 1 (1966): 66.
9. Peter Walker, *Moral Choices: Memory Desire and Imagination in Nineteenth-Century American Abolition* (Baton Rouge: Louisiana State, 1978), 295; Charles Rosenberg, "Sexuality, Class, and Role in 19th-Century America," *American Quarterly* 25, no. 2 (1973): 149.
10. Ronald G. Walters, "The Erotic South: Civilization and Sexuality in American Abolitionism," *American Quarterly* 25, no. 2 (1973): 178–179, 186.
11. Ibid., 180.
12. Walker, *Moral Choices,* 297.
13. Walters, "The Erotic South," 193.
14. Rosenberg, "Sexuality, Class, and Role in 19th-Century America," 135–137, 140–141.
15. Ibid., 295.
16. Ibid., 149.
17. Ibid., 144.
18. James Horton and Lois Horton, *In Hope of Liberty: Culture, Community and Protest among Northern Free Blacks, 1700–1860* (New York: Oxford University Press, 1997), 54.
19. Ibid., 543.
20. Ibid., 722.
21. Toni Morrison, *Playing in the Dark: Whiteness and the Literary Imagination* (New York: Random House, 1993), 17.
22. Hildreth, introduction, vii.
23. Ibid., vii.
24. Ibid., viii.
25. Richard Hildreth, *The Slave: or, Memoirs of Archy Moore* (Boston: John H. Eastburn, 1836; reprint, Upper Saddle River, N.J.: Gregg Press, 1968), part 1, 4.
26. Werner Sollors, *Neither Black nor White yet Both: Thematic Explorations of Interracial Literature* (New York: Oxford University Press, 1997), 6.

27. Hildreth, *The Slave: or, Memoirs of Archy Moore,* part 1, 57.

28. Ibid., part 2, 46.

29. Ibid., part 2, 9.

30. Anne Dalke, "Original Vice: The Political Implications of Incest in the Early American Novel," *Early American Literature* 23, no. 2 (1988): 188–189.

31. David S. Reynolds, *Beneath the American Renaissance: The Subversive Imagination in the Age of Emerson and Melville* (New York: Knopf, 1988), 223, 73–79.

32. Ibid., 74.

33. Ibid., 221.

34. Karen Halttunen, "Humanitarianism and the Pornography of Pain in Anglo-American Culture," *American Historical Review* 100, no. 2 (1995): 304, 317.

35. Ibid., 315, 324.

36. Ibid., 325.

37. Ibid., 326.

38. Steven Marcus, *The Other Victorians: A Study of Sexuality and Pornography in Mid-Nineteenth-Century England* (New York: Basic Books, 1964), 245.

39. H. L. Malchow, *Gothic Images of Race in Nineteenth-Century Britain* (Stanford: Stanford University Press, 1996), 4.

40. Ibid., 5.

41. Halttunen, "Humanitarianism and the Pornography of Pain," 311.

42. Hildreth, *The Slave: or, Memoirs of Archy Moore,* part 1, 1.

43. Ibid., 87.

44. Ibid.

45. Gerald Early, "'A servant of servants shall he be . . .': Paternalism and Millennialism in American Slavery Literature, 1850–1859" (Ph.D. diss., Cornell University, 1982), 115.

46. Hildreth, *The Slave: or, Memoirs of Archy Moore,* part 1, 53–54.

47. Ibid., part 2, 9.

48. Ibid., part 1, 114, 115–116.

49. Sollors, *Neither Black Nor White Yet Both,* 319.

50. Rosenberg, "Sexuality, Class, and Role in 19th-Century America," 144.

51. Nicholas Canaday Jr., "The Anti-Slavery Novel Prior to 1852 and Hildreth's *The Slave* (1836)," *CLA Journal* 27, no. 2 (1973): 185–186.

52. Hildreth, *The Slave: or, Memoirs of Archy Moore,* part 1, 10.

53. Ibid., part 2, 93.

54. Ibid., part 2, 72.

55. Ibid., part 2, 71.

56. Ibid., part 2, 83.

57. Ibid., part 2, 94.

58. Canaday, "The Anti-Slavery Novel Prior to 1852," 184.

59. Hildreth, *The Slave: or, Memoirs of Archy Moore,* part 2, 76.

60. Ibid., 96.

61. Ibid., 114.

62. Ibid., 117–118.

63. Ibid., 123.

64. Canaday, "The Anti-Slavery Novel Prior to 1852," 186.

65. Hildreth, *The Slave: or, Memoirs of Archy Moore,* part 2, 123.

66. Slotkin, *Regeneration through Violence,* 5.

67. Hildreth, *The Slave: or, Memoirs of Archy Moore,* part 2, 153.

3. Reconstructing America in Lydia Maria Child's *A Romance of the Republic* and Frances E. W. Harper's *Minnie's Sacrifice*

1. Eric Foner, *A Short History of Reconstruction, 1863–1877* (New York: Harper and Row, 1990), 115.

2. Frances Smith Foster, introduction to *Nellie Brown, or the Jealous Wife and Other Sketches* (Lincoln: University of Nebraska, 1996), ix.

3. Frances E. W. Harper, *Minnie's Sacrifice; Sowing and Reaping; Trial and Triumph: Three Rediscovered Novels,* ed. Frances Smith Foster (Boston: Beacon Press, 1994), 3.

4. For a discussion of Harper's use of the Moses theme, see Frances Smith Foster, introduction to *Minnie's Sacrifice* (Boston: Beacon Press, 1994), xxx; see also Frances Smith Foster, ed., *A Brighter Coming Day: A Frances Ellen Watkins Harper Reader* (New York: Feminist Press at The City University of New York, 1990), 135–136.

5. Patricia G. Holland, Milton Meltzer, and Francine Krasno, eds., *Collected Correspondence of Lydia Maria Child, 1817–1880* (Millwood, N.Y.: Kraus Microform, 1980), fiche 67, letter 1789.

6. Carolyn Karcher, *The First Woman in the Republic: A Cultural Biography of Lydia Maria Child* (Durham: Duke University Press, 1994), 510.

7. Lydia Maria Child, *A Romance of the Republic* (Lexington: University of Kentucky Press, 1997), 4.

8. Ibid., 127, 339.

9. Bruce Mills, *Cultural Reformations: Lydia Maria Child and the Literature of Reform* (Athens: University of Chicago Press, 1944), 131.

10. Lydia Maria Child, "The Quadroons," in Child, *Fact and Fiction: A Collection of Stories* (New York: C. S. Francis & Co., 1847).

11. Andrea K. Newlyn, "Form and Ideology in Transracial Narratives: *Pudd'nhead Wilson* and *A Romance of the Republic,*" *Narrative* 8, no. 1 (2000): 43–65.

12. Child, *A Romance of the Republic,* 4.

13. Ibid., 18.

14. Ibid., 8–9.

15. Karcher, *The First Woman in the Republic,* 523.

16. Child, *A Romance of the Republic,* 130.

17. Ibid., 135.

18. Ibid., 433.

19. Dana Nelson, introduction to Child, *A Romance of the Republic,* ix–x.

20. Child, *A Romance of the Republic,* 10.

21. Ibid., 103.

22. Ibid., 209.

23. Ibid., 151.

24. Karcher, *The First Woman in the Republic,* 321.

25. Butler's trilogy includes *Dawn* (1987), *Adulthood Rites* (1988), and *Imago* (1989). For a discussion of the relationship between Butler's representation of hybridity and nineteenth-century mixed-race fiction, see my epilogue.

26. Child, *A Romance of the Republic,* 432.

27. Karcher, *First Woman of the Republic,* 523–526.

28. Child, *A Romance of the Republic,* 420.

29. Ibid., 433.

30. Karcher, *The First Woman in the Republic,* 525.

31. Nelson, introduction to Child, *A Romance of the Republic,* xv.

32. Child, *A Romance of the Republic,* 419.

33. Ibid., 398.

34. Ibid., 393.

35. Ibid., 434.

36. Ibid., 422, 421.

37. Ibid., 433.

38. Though the chapter that includes Minnie's death is missing, in the epilogue Harper indicates that her murder was committed by the Ku Klux Klan.

39. Harper, *Minnie's Sacrifice,* 3.

40. Ibid., 91.

41. Ibid., 5.

42. A literary adaptation of the Moses story was not new to Harper. Prior to the publication of *Minnie's Sacrifice,* she published the long poem *Moses: A Story of the Nile* (originally published as a single volume), another poem called "The Burial of Moses" (1856), and an essay on Moses entitled "Our Greatest Want" (1859). These selections have been published in Foster, ed., *A Brighter Coming Day,* 138, 77, 102. According to Foster, Harper, like many African Americans, was inspired by the story of Moses because of the parallels between the plight of African Americans and the plight of the Jews in the Bible. The story also resonated with her own life as an orphan who had escaped enslavement, was adopted by a more privileged class, and dedicated her life to the underprivileged. While the exact date of the first publication of *Moses: A Story of the Nile* is unknown, Frances Smith Foster notes that the second edition of the poem was published in 1869 and the first edition probably was not created before 1865. Foster, ed., *A Brighter Coming Day,* 136.

43. Foner, *A Short History of Reconstruction,* 42.

44. Ibid.

45. William Still, *The Underground Rail Road: A Record of Facts, Authentic Narrative, Letters, &c.* (1872; reprint, Chicago: Johnson Publishing Co., 1970), 800.

46. Harper, *Minnie's Sacrifice,* 72.

47. Harper's letters written while lecturing in the South during Reconstruction reflect this sentiment. In an 1871 letter to William Still, Harper tells the story of a slave woman who was raped by her master. According to Harper, the woman was poorly fed and resorted to prostitution for food. Harper asks: "Had not hunger and cruelty and prostitution done their work, and left her an entire wreck for life? It seems not. Freedom came, and with it dawned a new era upon that poor, overshadowed, and sin-darkened life" (Still, *The Underground Rail Road,* 808). According to Harper, the woman found a job and received wages, which she used to educate herself and become a schoolteacher. Eventually the woman was able to lend money to her former mistress. This story of renewal encapsulates the central theme of Harper's novel. It is significant that the woman's rebirth involves both economic prosperity and educational and moral development, all forms of progress that Harper hoped would come to African Americans.

48. Harper, *Minnie's Sacrifice,* 78.

49. Ibid., 70.

50. Nancy Bentley, "White Slaves: The Mulatto Hero in Antebellum Fiction," *American Literature* 65, no. 3 (1993): 505. According to Bentley, "[T]he tragic Mulatta is granted her most pronounced symbolic power by virtue of her worldly suffering—her sexual exploitation, and the betrayals and abuse she endures usually find physical expression in sui-

cide or fatal suffering." Bentley contends that ultimately the suffering of mulattas is a means through which they achieve spiritual transcendence, while male near-white characters are not subjected to the same criteria. In fact, white male bodies, including near-whites, are often the agents of violence, such as Stowe's George. While Bentley's theory sheds light on how mulatto characters expose the culture, her theory does not take into account the sexualization of some of these characters or the figure of the suffering mixed-race male character, such as Frank J. Webb's Clarence of *The Garies and Their Friends* (1857).

51. Lydia Maria Child, *Fact and Fiction: A Collection of Stories* (New York: C. S. Francis & Co., 1847), 71.

52. Harper, *Minnie's Sacrifice,* 89.

53. Ibid., 36.

54. Ibid.

55. My ideas on Louis's representative power were greatly influenced by Frances Smith Foster's spring 1999 seminar, "Heroic Slaves and Tragic Mulattos," at Emory University.

56. Kimberly A. C. Wilson, "The Function of the 'Fair' Mulatto: Complexion, Audience, and Mediation in Frances Harper's *Iola Leroy,*" *Cimarron Review* 106 (1994): 105.

4. Doubles in Eden in George Washington Cable's *The Grandissimes*

1. George E. Marcus, "'What did he reckon would become of the other half if he killed his half?': Doubled, Divided, and Crossed Selves in *Pudd'nhead Wilson;* or Mark Twain as Cultural Critic in His Own Times and Ours," in *Mark Twain's Pudd'nhead Wilson,* ed. Susan Gillman and Forrest G. Robinson (Durham, N.C.: Duke University Press, 1990), 193.

2. Ibid., 195.

3. Ibid., 197–198.

4. Stanley Brodwin offers an extensive discussion of the significance of Eden in *Pudd'nhead Wilson* in "Blackness and the Adamic Myth in Mark Twain's *Pudd'nhead Wilson,*" *Texas Studies in Literature and Language* 15, no. 1 (Spring 1973): 167–175.

5. Mark Twain, *Pudd'nhead Wilson and Those Extraordinary Twins* (New York: W.W. Norton & Company, 1980), 3.

6. Ibid., 4.

7. My interpretation of this passage is greatly influenced by Toni Morrison's *Playing in the Dark* (New York: Random House, 1992). She writes, "Nothing highlighted freedom—if it did not in fact create it—like slavery" (38).

8. Shelley Fisher Fishkin, "Race and Culture at the Century's End: A Social Context for *Pudd'nhead Wilson,*" *Essays in Arts and Sciences* 19 (May 1990): 2.

9. Marcus, "'What did he reckon would become of the other half?'" 195.

10. George Washington Cable, *Old Creole Days* (Miami: Mnemosyne Publishing Co., 1969). "Tité Poulette" was originally published in *Scribner's Monthly* in 1874. This short story was also included in Cable's collection *Old Creole Days,* originally published in 1879.

11. Anna Shannon Elfenbein, *Women on the Color Line: Evolving Stereotypes and the Writings of George Washington Cable, Grace King, Kate Chopin* (Charlottesville: University Press of Virginia, 1989), 37.

12. Barbara Ladd, *Nationalism and the Color Line in George W. Cable, Mark Twain, and William Faulkner* (Baton Rouge: Louisiana State Press, 1996), 50.

13. George Washington Cable, "My Politics," in *The Negro Question: A Selection of Writings on Civil Rights in the South,* ed. Arlin Turner (New York: Doubleday, 1958), 14.

14. For a comparison of the conflict between Creoles and Americans in 1803 and the U.S. North–South conflict in relation to Cable's novel, see John Clemen, *George Washington Cable Revisited* (New York: Simon & Schuster, 1996), 61–62.

15. For a discussion of the similarities between Frowenfeld and Cable, see Louis D. Rubin Jr., *George Washington Cable: The Life and Times of a Southern Heretic* (New York: Western Publishing Co., 1969), 94.

16. George Washington Cable, *The Grandissimes: A Story of Creole Life* (Athens: University of Georgia Press, 1988), 305.

17. Lawrence Berkove, "The Free Man of Color in *The Grandissimes* and Works by Harris and Mark Twain," *Southern Quarterly* 18, no. 4 (1980): 60.

18. While the exact familial relationship between Aurora and Palmyre is never revealed, Aurora's father, in a letter to Agricola, reveals that she is biologically related to the De Grapions. The intimacy of this revelation suggests that it would be inappropriate for a party other than the father of Palmyre to reveal it. Cable, *The Grandissimes,* 176.

19. Ibid., 60.

20. Ibid., 180.

21. Ibid., 188.

22. Suzanne Jones, foreword to *The Grandissimes: A Story of Creole Life* (Athens: University of Georgia Press, 1988), x.

23. Cable, *The Grandissimes,* 156.

24. Ibid., 8, 9.

25. Ibid., 9.

26. Ibid., 9.

27. Ibid., 117.

28. Ibid., 37.

29. Ibid., 156.

30. Ibid., 156.

31. Ibid., 196.

32. Ibid., 196.

33. Ibid., 196.

34. Ibid., 318.

35. Ibid., 19.

36. Ibid., 59–60.

37. Elfenbein, *Women on the Color Line,* 54.

38. Cable, *The Grandissimes,* 176.

39. Ibid., 255.

40. Ibid., 135–136.

41. Ibid., 156.

42. Rubin, *George Washington Cable,* 91.

43. Cable, *The Grandissimes,* 135.

44. Ibid., 134.

45. Ibid., 136.

46. Ibid., 201.

47. Ibid., 201.

48. Ibid., 201.

49. Ibid., 71.

50. For a discussion of Cable's views on miscegenation, see Ladd, *Nationalism and the Color Line,* 41–42.

51. Cable, *The Grandissimes,* 71.

52. James R. Frisby Jr., "New Orleans Writers and the Negro: George Washington Cable, Grace King, Ruth McEnery Stuart, Kate Chopin, and Lafcadio Hearn, 1870–1900" (Ph.D. diss., Emory University, 1972), 71.

53. Cable, *The Grandissimes,* 55.

54. Ibid., 197.

55. John Clemen, *George Washington Cable Revisited* (New York: Simon and Schuster, 1996), 74.

56. Cable, *The Grandissimes,* 195–196.

57. As Clemen points out, the intensity of Palmyre's anger is also overtly erotic. *George Washington Cable Revisited,* 71.

58. Cable, *The Grandissimes,* 175.

59. Ibid., 9.

60. Ibid., 321.

61. Ibid., 264.

5. "I will gladly share with them my richer heritage"

1. Using Chesnutt's letters, Charles Hackenberry estimates that *Mandy Oxendine* may have been started in 1894 and completed in 1896, though it possibly could have existed in one form or another as early as 1889. Charles Hackenberry, introduction to *Mandy Oxendine* (Urbana: University of Illinois Press, 1997), xiv–xvii; however, according to William L. Andrews, the story was probably written in 1893 and revised in 1894 or 1895 before submission to the *Atlantic,* which rejected it. William L. Andrews, *The Literary Career of Charles W. Chesnutt* (Baton Rouge: Louisiana State University Press, 1980), 145.

2. Frances E. W. Harper, "A Factor in Human Progress," *African Methodist Episcopal Church Review* 2 (1885): 14–18; quoted in Frances Smith Foster, ed., *A Brighter Coming Day: A Frances Ellen Watkins Harper Reader* (New York: Feminist Press at The City University of New York, 1990), 276.

3. For a discussion of black self-help organizations after Reconstruction, see August Meier, *Negro Thought in America, 1880–1915: Racial Ideologies in the Age of Booker T. Washington* (Ann Arbor: University of Michigan Press, 1966), 121–138.

4. John Hope Franklin and Alfred A. Moss Jr., *From Slavery to Freedom* (New York: McGraw-Hill, 1994), 239.

5. Frances E. W. Harper, *Iola Leroy, or Shadows Uplifted* (New York: Mentor, 1992), 88.

6. Charles Chesnutt, *Mandy Oxendine,* ed. Charles Hackenberry (Urbana: University of Illinois Press, 1997), 28.

7. For a thorough analysis of the relationship between freedom and education for African Americans before and after the Civil War, see James Anderson, *The Education of Blacks in the South, 1860–1935* (Chapel Hill: University of North Carolina, 1988).

8. Faustine C. Jones-Wilson, ed., *Encyclopedia of African-American Education* (West Port, Conn.: Greenwood Press, 1996), 347–348.

9. James D. Anderson, *The Education of Blacks in the South, 1860–1935* (Chapel Hill: University of North Carolina, 1988), 7, 16.

10. Eric Foner, *A Short History of Reconstruction, 1863–1877* (New York: Harper and Row, 1990), 43–44.

11. Anderson, *The Education of Blacks in the South,* 5–7.

12. Ibid., 28.

13. Foner, *A Short History of Reconstruction,* 44.

14. Anderson, *The Education of Blacks in the South,* 23.

15. Ibid., 12–15.

16. Ibid., 13.

17. Henry Allen Bullock, *A History of Negro Education in the South from 1619 to the Present* (Cambridge: Harvard University Press, 1967), 173.

18. Anderson, *The Education of Blacks in the South,* 253–254.

19. Ibid., 111.

20. Ibid.

21. Kevin Gaines, "Assimilationist Minstrelsy as Racial Uplift Ideology," *American Quarterly* (1993): 345–346.

22. Foner, *A Short History of Reconstruction,* 44.

23. Joel Williamson, *New People: Miscegenation and Mulattoes in the United States* (New York: Free Press, 1980), 130.

24. Foner, *A Short History of Reconstruction,* 44–45.

25. Williamson, *New People,* 88.

26. Foster, ed., *A Brighter Coming Day,* 9.

27. Andrews, *The Literary Career of Charles W. Chesnutt,* 3, 8.

28. Hackenberry, introduction, xvi–xvii.

29. William Still, *The Underground Rail Road: A Record of Facts, Authentic Narrative, Letters, &c.* (1872; reprint, Chicago: Johnson Publishing Co., 1970), 786; Foster, ed., *A Brighter Coming Day,* 9; Anderson, *The Education of Blacks in the South,* 12–15.

30. Richard Brodhead, ed., *The Journals of Charles Chesnutt* (Durham: Duke University Press, 1993), 157.

31. Carla Peterson, "Further Liftings of the Veil: Gender, Class, and Labor in Frances E. W. Harper," in *Listening to Silences: New Essays in Feminist Criticism,* ed. Elaine Hedges and Shelly Fisher Fishkin (New York: Oxford University Press, 1994), 102.

32. Harper, *Iola Leroy,* 111.

33. Hazel Carby, *Reconstructing Womanhood: The Emergence of Afro-American Women Novelists* (New York: Oxford University Press, 1987), 78.

34. Marilyn Elkins argues that there is no hierarchy of class or color among the women characters in Harper. Marilyn Elkins, "Reading beyond Conventions A Look at Frances E. W. Harper's *Iola Leroy, or Shadows Uplifted,*" *American Literary Realism* 22, no. 2 (1990): 44–53. In addition, John Ernest contends that Harper suggests that education is a mutual effort, not just the socialization of one culture as defined by another. John Ernest, "From Mysteries to Histories: Cultural Pedagogy in Frances E. W. Harper's *Iola Leroy,*" *American Literature* 64 (1992): 497–518.

35. Barbara Christian, "Shadows Uplifted," in *Feminist Criticism and Social Change,* ed. Judith Newton and Deborah Rosenfelt (New York: Methuen, 1985), 206.

36. Vashti Lewis, "The Near-White Female in Frances Ellen Harper's *Iola Leroy,*" *Phylon* 45, no. 4 (1984): 322.

37. Deborah McDowell, *"The Changing Same": Black Women's Literature, Criticism, and Theory* (Bloomington: Indiana University Press, 1995), 39.

38. Harper, *Iola Leroy,* 146.

39. Chesnutt, *Mandy Oxendine,* 46.
40. Ibid., 46.
41. Ibid., 29.
42. Ibid., 23.
43. Ibid., 10.
44. Ibid., 9–10.
45. Ibid., 10.
46. According to Arlene Elder, despite Chesnutt's lifelong friendship with Booker T. Washington, he agreed more with W. E. B. DuBois's theories that supported liberal education. While Chesnutt did not object to industrial education, he contended that there was no single plan that would solve the problems of all blacks and that African Americans should also have the opportunity for liberal education and political advancement. Arlene Elder, "Chesnutt on Washington: An Essential Ambivalence," *Phylon* 38 (1977): 1–8. Though Washington was clearly in the minority among black educators in his support of industrial education for blacks, the congruence between manual education and the need for wage labor in the South contributed to Washington's preeminence as the designated black leader in the field of education. As James Anderson has noted, by 1881, many white southerners had begun to recognize that while the gains of black education could not be undone, perhaps black educational methods could be adapted to meet the need for manual labor in the South. Anderson, *The Education of Blacks in the South,* 31.
47. Elkins, "Reading beyond Conventions," 46.
48. Chesnutt, *Mandy Oxendine,* 29.
49. Ibid., 14.
50. Ibid., 15.
51. Ibid., 80.
52. Ibid., 100–101.
53. Ibid., 110.
54. Foster, ed., *A Brighter Coming Day,* 280.
55. Chesnutt, *Mandy Oxendine,* 81–82. Richard Brodhead has noted that Chesnutt's journals exhibit ambivalence about the culture of rural southern uneducated blacks. While Chesnutt is sometimes condescending, he later describes his interest in black popular culture. However, Chesnutt often determined the value of black art forms by their relevance to Western standards. For more see, Richard Brodhead, introduction to Brodhead, ed., *The Journals of Charles Chesnutt,* 23–24.
56. Brodhead, introduction, 16.
57. Ibid.
58. Foster, ed., *A Brighter Coming Day,* 6–8.
59. Ibid., 10.
60. Harper, *Iola Leroy,* 203.

Epilogue

1. "1850: Circular to the Marshals," point 6, in Steven Ruggles and Matthew Sobek et al., *Integrated Public Use Microdata Series: Version 3.0* (Minneapolis: Historical Census Projects, University of Minnesota, 2003), available online at www.ipums.umn.edu/usa/voliii/inst1850.html.
2. Melissa Nobles, *Shades of Citizenship: Race and the Census in Modern Politics* (Stanford: Stanford University Press, 2000), 1.

3. Ibid., 35–37.

4. Ibid., 35–43. Nobles argues that historical analyses of the addition of the category "mulatto" have relied too heavily on census bureau documents that suggest that demographic changes determined the addition. Examining Senate debates about the census, she demonstrates that the addition of the category was profoundly influenced by polygenists who wanted to measure the lifespans of mixed-race peoples to support their theory of separate origins.

5. "1890 Census: Instructions to Enumerators," Color, Sex, and Age, point 4, in Ruggles and Sobek et al., *Integrated Public Use Microdata Series,* available online at www.ipums.umn.edu/usa/voliii/inst1890.html.

6. "1930 Census: Enumerator Instructions," Personal Description, point 141, in Ruggles and Sobek et al., *Integrated Public Use Microdata Series,* available online at www.ipums.umn.edu/usa/voliii/inst1930.html.

7. Michele Osherow, "The Dawn of a New Lilith: Revisionary Mythmaking in Women's Science Fiction," *National Women's Studies Association Journal* 12, no. 1 (Spring 2000): 78.

Bibliography

Anderson, James. *The Education of Blacks in the South, 1860–1935.* Chapel Hill: University of North Carolina Press, 1988.

Andrews, William. *The Literary Career of Charles W. Chesnutt.* Baton Rouge: Louisiana State University Press, 1980.

Aptheker, Herbert. *Abolitionism: A Revolutionary Movement.* Boston: G. K. Hall & Co., 1989.

Arbery, Glenn Cannon. "Victims of Likeness: Quadroons and Octoroons in Southern Fiction." *Southern Review* 25, no. 1 (1989): 52–71.

Arvin, Newton. "Introduction to *The Grandissimes.*" In *Critical Essays on George Washington Cable,* ed. Arlin Turner. Boston: G. K. Hall and Co., 1980.

Babb, Valerie. *Whiteness Visible.* New York: New York University Press, 1998.

Baker, Houston A., Jr. *Workings of the Spirit: The Poetics of Afro-American Women's Writing.* Chicago: University of Chicago Press, 1991.

Bentley, Nancy. "White Slaves: The Mulatto Hero in Antebellum Fiction." *American Literature* 65, no. 3 (1993): 501–522.

Berkove, Lawrence. "The Free Man of Color in *The Grandissimes* and Works by Harris and Twain." *Southern Quarterly* 18, no. 4 (1980): 60–73.

Berlant, Lauren. "National Brands/National Body: Imitation of Life." In *Comparative American Identities: Race, Sex, and Nationality in the Modern Text,* ed. Hortense J. Spillers. New York: Routledge, 1991.

Birnbaum, Michele. "Racial Hysteria: Female Pathology and Race Politics in Frances Harper's *Iola Leroy* and W. D. Howell's an *Imperative Duty.*" *African American Review* 33, no. 1 (1999): 7–23.

Bost, Suzanne. "Fluidity without Postmodernism: Michelle Cliff and the 'Tragic Mulatta' Tradition." *African American Review* 32, no. 4 (1998): 673–689.

Brandstater, Evan. "Uncle Tom and Archy Moore: The Antislavery Novel as Ideological Symbol." *American Quarterly* 26, no. 2 (1974): 164–175.

Brodhead, Richard. Introduction to *The Journals of Charles Chesnutt,* ed. Richard Brodhead. Durham, N.C.: Duke University Press, 1993.

———, ed. *The Journals of Charles Chesnutt.* Durham, N.C.: Duke University Press, 1993.

Brodwin, Stanley. "Blackness and the Adamic Myth in Mark Twain's *Pudd'nhead Wilson.*" *Texas Studies in Literature and Language* 15, no. 1 (1973): 167–175.

Brown, Sterling. *The Negro in American Fiction.* Washington, D.C.: The Association in Negro Folk Education, 1937.

Brown, Sterling A., Arthur P. Davis, and Ulysses Lee, eds. *The Negro Caravan.* New York: Arno Press, 1970.

Bullock, Henry Allen. *A History of Negro Education in the South from 1619 to the Present.* Cambridge, Mass.: Harvard University Press, 1967.

Butcher, Phillip. *George Washington Cable.* New York: Twayne Publishers, 1962.

Cable, George Washington. *The Grandissimes: A Story of Creole Life.* 1880. Reprint, Athens: University of Georgia Press, 1988.

———. "My Politics." In *The Negro Question: A Selection of Writings on Civil Rights in the South,* ed. Arlin Turner. New York: Doubleday, 1958.

———. "The Silent South." In *The Negro Question: A Selection of Writing on Civil Rights in the South,* ed. Arlin Turner. New York: Doubleday, 1958.

Canaday, Nicholas, Jr. "The Anti-Slavery Novel Prior to 1852 and Hildreth's *The Slave* (1836)." *CLA Journal* 27, no. 2 (1973): 175–191.

Carby, Hazel. *Reconstructing Womanhood: The Emergence of Afro-American Women Novelists.* New York: Oxford University Press, 1987.

Chesnutt, Charles. *Mandy Oxendine.* Ed. Charles Hackenberry. Urbana: University of Illinois Press, 1997.

Child, Lydia Maria. *Fact and Fiction: A Collection of Stories.* New York: C. S. Francis & Co., 1847.

———. *A Romance of the Republic.* Lexington: University of Kentucky Press, 1997.

Christian, Barbara. "Shadows Uplifted." In *Feminist Criticism and Social Change,* ed. Judith Newton and Deborah Rosenfelt. New York: Methuen, 1985.

Clemen, John. *George Washington Cable Revisited.* New York: Simon and Schuster, 1996.

Clymer, Jeffory A. "Race and the Protocol of American Citizenship in William Dean Howell's *An Imperative Duty.*" *American Literary Realism* 30, no. 3 (1998): 31–52.

Cooper, James Fenimore. *The Last of the Mohicans, a Narrative of 1757.* 1826. Reprint, New York: J. G. Gregory, 1864.

———. *The Travelling Bachelor; or, Notions of the American.* New York: Stinger and Townsend, 1852.

Dalke, Anne. "Original Vice: The Political Implications of Incest in the Early American Novel." *Early American Literature* 23, no. 2 (1988): 188–201.

Dearborn, Mary. *Pocahontas's Daughters: Gender and Ethnicity in American Culture.* New York: Oxford University Press, 1986.

Dekker, George, and John P. McWilliams. *Fenimore Cooper: The Critical Heritage.* London: Routledge & Kegan Paul, 1973.

Drinnon, Richard. *Facing West: The Metaphysics of Indian-Hating and Empire-Building.* Minneapolis: University of Minnesota Press, 1980.

Ducille, Ann. *The Coupling Convention: Sex, Text, and Tradition in Black Women's Fiction.* New York: Oxford University Press, 1993.

Dumond, Dwight Lowell. *Antislavery: The Crusade for Freedom in America.* Ann Arbor: University of Michigan Press, 1961.

Early, Gerald. "'A servant of servants shall he be . . .': Paternalism and Millenialism in American Slavery Literature, 1850–1859." Ph.D. diss., Cornell University, 1982.

Elder, Arlene. "Chesnutt on Washington: An Essential Ambivalence." *Phylon* 38 (1977): 1–8.

Elfenbein, Anna Shannon. *Women on the Color Line: Evolving Stereotypes and the Writings of George Washington Cable, Grace King, Kate Chopin.* Charlottesville: University Press of Virginia, 1989.

Elkins, Marilyn. "Reading beyond Conventions: A Look at Frances E. W. Harper's *Iola Leroy, or Shadows Uplifted.*" *American Literary Realism* 22, no. 2 (1990): 44–53.

Ernest, John. "From Mysteries to Histories: Cultural Pedagogy in Frances E. W. Harper's *Iola Leroy.*" *American Literature* 64 (1992): 497–518.

Evans, Williams. "French-English Literary Dialect in *The Grandissimes.*" In *Critical Essays on George W. Cable,* ed. Arlin Turner. Boston: G. K. Hall and Co., 1980.

Fiedler, Leslie. *Love and Death in the American Novel.* New York: Criterion, 1960.

Fishkin, Shelley Fisher. "Race and Culture at the Century's End: A Social Context for *Pudd'nhead Wilson.*" *Essays in Arts and Sciences* 19 (May 1990): 1–27.

Foner, Eric. *A Short History of Reconstruction, 1863–1877.* New York: Harper and Row, 1990.

Foster, Frances Smith, ed. *A Brighter Coming Day: A Frances Ellen Watkins Harper Reader.* New York: Feminist Press at The City University of New York, 1990.

———. Introduction to *A Brighter Coming Day: A Frances Ellen Watkins Harper Reader,* ed. Frances Smith Foster. New York: Feminist Press at The City University of New York, 1990.

———. Introduction to *Nellie Brown; or, The Jealous Wife, with Other Sketches,* by Thomas Detter. 1871. Reprint, Lincoln: University of Nebraska Press, 1996.

Franklin, John Hope, and Alfred A. Moss Jr. *From Slavery to Freedom.* New York: McGraw-Hill, 1994.

Frisby, James R., Jr. "New Orleans Writers and the Negro: George Washington Cable, Grace King, Ruth McEnery Stuart, Kate Chopin, and Lafcadio Hearn, 1870–1900." Ph.D. diss., Emory University, 1972.

Gaines, Kevin. "Assimilationist Minstrelsy as Racial Uplift Ideology." *American Quarterly* 45, no. 3 (1993): 341–369.

Garrison, William Lloyd. *Thoughts on African Colonization.* 1832. Reprint, New York: Arno Press, 1969.

Gillette, William. *Retreat from Reconstruction, 1869–1879.* Baton Rouge: Louisiana State University Press, 1979.

Green, Beriah. *Sketches of the Life and Writings of James Gillespie Birney.* Utica: Jackson and Chaplin, 1844.

Guilds, John Caldwell. Introduction to *The Yemassee: A Romance of Carolina,* by William Gilmore Simms. Fayetteville: University of Arkansas Press, 1994.

Haberly, David T. "Women and Indians: *The Last of the Mohicans* and the Captivity Tradition." *American Quarterly* 28 (1976): 431–443.

Hackenberry, Charles. Introduction to *Mandy Oxendine,* by Charles Chesnutt. Urbana: University of Illinois Press, 1997.

Halttunen, Karen. "Humanitarianism and the Pornography of Pain in Anglo-American Culture." *American Historical Review* 100, no. 2 (1995): 303–334.

Harper, Frances E. W. *Iola Leroy, or Shadows Uplifted.* 1892. Reprint, New York: Mentor, 1992.

———. *Minnie's Sacrifice; Sowing and Reaping; Trial and Triumph: Three Rediscovered Novels.* Ed. Frances Smith Foster. Boston: Beacon Press, 1994.

Hershberger, Mary. "Mobilizing Women, Anticipating Abolition: The Struggle against Indian Removal in the 1830's." *Journal of American History* 86, no. 1 (1999): 15–40.

Hildreth, Richard. Introduction to *Archy Moore, The White Slave; or, Memoirs of a Fugitive,* by Richard Hildreth. New York: Miller, Orton and Mulligan, 1856. Reprint, New York: Negro Universities Press, 1969.

———. *The Slave; or, Memoirs of Archy Moore.* Boston: John H. Eastburn, 1836. Reprint, Upper Saddle River, N.J.: Gregg Press, 1968.

Holland, Patricia G., Milton Meltzer, and Francine Krasno, eds. *The Collected Correspondence of Lydia Maria Child, 1917–1880.* Millwood, N.Y.: Kraus Microform, 1980.

Horton, James, and Lois Horton. *In Hope of Liberty: Culture, Community and Protest among Northern Free Blacks, 1700–1860.* New York: Oxford University Press, 1997.

Howells, William Dean. *An Imperative Duty.* New York: Harper & Brothers, 1892.

Jefferson, Thomas. *Writings.* New York: Viking Press, 1984.

Jehlen, Myrah. "The Ties That Bind: Race and Sex in *Pudd'nhead Wilson.*" *American Literary History* 2, no. 1 (1990): 39–55.

Jones, Suzanne. Foreword to *The Grandissimes: A Story of Creole Life*, by George Washington Cable. Athens: University of Georgia Press, 1988.

Jones-Wilson, Faustine C., ed. *Encyclopedia of African-American Education.* Westport, Conn.: Greenwood Press, 1996.

Jordan, Winthrop. *White over Black: Attitudes toward the Negro, 1550–1812.* Chapel Hill: University of North Carolina Press, 1968.

Karcher, Carolyn. *The First Woman in the Republic: A Cultural Biography of Lydia Maria Child.* Durham, N.C.: Duke University Press, 1994.

Kerber, Linda. "The Abolitionist Perception of the Indian." *Journal of American History* 62, no. 2 (1975): 271–295.

Kinney, James. *Amalgamation! Race, Sex, and Rhetoric in the Nineteenth-Century American Novel.* Westport, Conn.: Greenwood Press, 1985.

Ladd, Barbara. *Nationalism and the Color Line in George W. Cable, Mark Twain, and William Faulkner.* Baton Rouge: Louisiana State Press, 1996.

Lewis, R. W. B. *The American Adam.* Chicago: University of Chicago Press, 1955.

Lewis, Vashti. "The Near-White Female in Frances Ellen Harper's *Iola Leroy.*" *Phylon* 45, no. 4 (1984): 314–322.

Madison, James. *Letters and Other Writings of James Madison.* Philadelphia: J. B. Lippincott & Co., 1865.

Malchow, H. L. *Gothic Images of Race in Nineteenth-Century Britain.* Stanford, Calif.: Stanford University Press, 1996.

Malinowoski, Sharon, Anna Sheets, and Linda Schmittroth, eds. *Encyclopedia of Native American Tribes.* Vol. 1. Detroit: Gale Group, 1999.

Marcus, George E. "'What did he reckon would become of the other half if he killed his half?': Doubled, Divided, and Crossed Selves in *Pudd'nhead Wilson*; or Mark Twain as Cultural Critic in His Own Times and Ours." In *Mark Twain's Pudd'nhead Wilson,* ed. Susan Gillman and Forrest G. Robinson. Durham, N.C.: Duke University Press, 1990.

Marcus, Steven. *The Other Victorians: A Study of Sexuality and Pornography in Mid-Nineteenth-Century England.* New York: Basic Books, 1964.

Mayer, Henry. *All on Fire: William Lloyd Garrison and the Abolition of Slavery.* New York: St. Martin's Press, 1991.

Mayer, Magdalene. "Racial Perceptions in James Fenimore Cooper's *The Last of the Mohicans.*" In *Blurred Boundaries: Critical Essays on American Literature,* ed. Klaus Schmidt and David Sawyer. Frankfurt: Peter Lang, 1996.

McDowell, Deborah. *"The Changing Same": Black Women's Literature, Criticism, and Theory.* Bloomington: Indiana University Press, 1995.

Meier, August. *Negro Thought in America, 1880–1915: Racial Ideologies in the Age of Booker T. Washington.* Ann Arbor: University of Michigan Press, 1966.

Mills, Bruce. *Cultural Reformations: Lydia Maria Child and the Literature of Reform.* Athens: University of Georgia Press, 1994.

Morrison, Toni. *Playing in the Dark: Whiteness and the Literary Imagination.* New York: Random House, 1993.

Nelson, Dana. Introduction to *A Romance of the Republic,* by Lydia Maria Child. Lexington: University of Kentucky Press, 1997.

Nettels, Elsa. *Language, Race, and Class in Howell's America.* Lexington: University of Kentucky Press, 1988.

Newlyn, Andrea K. "Form and Ideology in Transracial Narratives: *Pudd'nhead Wilson* and *A Romance of the Republic.*" *Narrative* 8, no. 1 (2000): 43–65.

Nobles, Melissa. *Shades of Citizenship: Race and the Census in Modern Politics.* Stanford: Stanford University Press, 2000.

Osherow, Michelle. "The Dawn of a New Lilith: Revisionary Mythmaking in Women's Science Fiction." *National Women's Studies Association Journal* 12, no. 1 (Spring 2000): 68–83.

Pease, Donald. *Visionary Compacts: American Renaissance Writings in Cultural Context.* Madison: University of Wisconsin Press, 1987.

Peterson, Carla. "Further Liftings of the Veil: Gender, Class, and Labor in Frances E. W. Harper." In *Listening to Silences: New Essays in Feminist Criticism,* ed. Elaine Hedges and Shelly Fisher Fishkin. New York: Oxford University Press, 1994.

Porte, Joel. *The Romance in America: Studies in Cooper, Poe, Hawthorne, Melville, and James.* Middletown: Wesleyan University Press, 1969.

Porter, Carolyn. "Roxanna's Plot." In *Mark Twain's Pudd'nhead Wilson: Race Conflict, and Culture,* ed. Susan Gillman and Forrest G. Robinson. Durham, N.C.: Duke University Press, 1990.

Porter, Kenneth Wiggins. "Negroes and Seminole War, 1817–1818." *The Journal of Negro History* 36, no. 3 (1951): 249–280.

———. "Negroes and the Seminole Wars, 1835–1842." *Journal of Southern History* 30, no. 4 (1964): 427–450.

Reynolds, David S. *Beneath the American Renaissance: The Subversive Imagination in the Age of Emerson and Melville.* New York: Knopf, 1988.

Robinson, Forrest G. "Uncertain Borders: Race, Sex, and Civilization in *Last of the Mohicans.*" *Arizona Quarterly* 47, no. 1 (1991): 1–28.

Rosenberg, Charles. "Sexuality, Class, and Role in 19th-Century America." *American Quarterly* 25, no. 2 (1973): 131–153.

Rubin, Louis D., Jr. *George Washington Cable: The Life and Times of a Southern Heretic.* New York: Western Publishing, 1969.

Ruggles, Steven, Matthew Sobek, et al. *Integrated Public Use Microdata Series: Version 3.0.* Minneapolis: Historical Census Projects, University of Minnesota, 2003. Available online at http://www.ipums.umn.edu/usa.

Rusco, Elmer R. *"Good Time Coming?": Black Nevadans in the Nineteenth Century.* Westport, Conn.: Greenwood Press, 1975.

Sánchez-Eppler, Karen. *Touching Liberty: Abolition, Feminism, and the Politics of the Body.* Berkeley: University of California Press, 1993.

Satz, Ronald N. *American Indian Policy in the Jacksonian Era.* Lincoln: University of Nebraska Press, 1975.

Savage, William Sherman. *Blacks in the West.* Westport, Conn.: Greenwood Press, 1976.

Simms, William Gilmore. *The Yemassee: A Romance of Carolina.* Ed. John Caldwell Guilds. Fayetteville: University of Arkansas Press, 1994.

Slotkin, Richard. *Regeneration through Violence: The Mythology of the American Frontier, 1600–1860.* New York: Harper Collins, 1996.

Sollors, Werner. *Neither Black nor White yet Both: Thematic Explorations of Interracial Literature.* New York: Oxford University Press, 1997.

Staudenraus, P. J. *The African Colonization Movement, 1816–1865.* New York: Columbia University Press, 1961.

Still, William. *The Underground Rail Road: A Record of Facts, Authentic Narrative, Letters, &c.* 1872. Reprint, Chicago: Johnson Publishing Co., 1970.

Stokes, Mason. "Someone's in the Garden with Eve: Race, Religion, and the American Fall." *American Quarterly* 50, no. 4 (1998): 718–744.

Tocqueville, Alexis de. *Democracy in America.* 1935 and 1940. Reprint, New York: Knopf, 1984.

Tompkins, Jane. *Sensational Designs.* New York: Oxford University Press, 1985.

Turner, Arlin. "Mark Twain and the South: *Pudd'nhead Wilson.*" *Southern Review* 4 (1968): 493–519.

Twain, Mark. *Pudd'nhead Wilson and Those Extraordinary Twins.* 1894. Reprint, New York: W.W. Norton & Company, 1980.

Walker, Cheryl. *Indian Nation: Native American Literature and Nineteenth-Century Nationalisms.* Durham, N.C.: Duke University Press, 1997.

Walker, Peter. *Moral Choices: Memory, Desire, and Imagination in Nineteenth-Century American Abolition.* Baton Rouge: Louisiana State University Press, 1978.

Walters, Ronald G. "The Erotic South: Civilization and Sexuality in American Abolitionism." *American Quarterly* 25, no. 2 (1973): 177–201.

Warren, Kenneth W. *Black and White Strangers: Race and American Literary Realism.* Chicago: University of Chicago Press, 1993.

Williamson, Joel. *New People: Miscegenation and Mulattoes in the United States.* New York: Free Press, 1980.

Wilson, Kimberly A. C. "The Function of the 'Fair' Mulatto: Complexion, Audience, and Mediation in Frances Harper's *Iola Leroy.*" *Cimarron Review* 106 (January 1994): 104–113.

Woodson, Carter G. *The Negro in Our History.* Washington, D.C.: Associated Publishers, 1941.

Wright, J. Leitch, Jr. *Creeks & Seminoles: The Destruction of the Muscogulge People.* Lincoln: University of Nebraska Press, 1986.

Yellin, Jean Fagan. *Women and Sisters: The Antislavery Feminists in American Culture.* New Haven, Conn.: Yale University Press, 1989.

Young, Robert. *Domesticating Slavery: The Master Class in Georgia and South Carolina 1670–1837.* Chapel Hill: University of North Carolina Press, 1999.

Zanger, Jules. "The 'Tragic Octoroon' in Pre–Civil War Fiction." *American Quarterly* 18, no. 1 (1966): 63–70.

Index

abolitionism, 2, 6; and antiremoval movement, 9–10, 12–16; and Child, 49, 54; and Harper, 61, 63; literature of, 31, 38, 39, 47; and mulatto fiction, 32–33; and Native Americans, 7, 13–14; and power, 32, 38; and sexuality, 32–33
activism, 1, 110; and education, 91–92; vs. individualism, 100–103; in *Mandy Oxendine,* 103–104; of teachers, 93, 94–95, 98
Adams, John Quincy, 15
Adela the Octoroon (Hosmer), 65, 74
African Americans: as aliens, 10; and citizenship, 49–50; civil rights of, 21–22, 48; and colonization movement, 14; color of, 105–106; education of, 56–57, 59, 60, 61, 92–97, 109; exclusion from whiteness of, 11; hierarchy among, 59–60, 68–69, 81, 92, 96–98, 104, 105, 108, 109, 111, 130n34, 131n55; male, 48, 58, 72, 75, 87, 88, 89, 127n50; middle class, 69, 92; and Native Americans, 14, 15–16, 21–29; objectification of, 63, 89; patriarchy among, 72; as performers, 55–56; population of, 21; and Reconstruction, 48; and Seminoles, 14–15. *See also* blackness; communities, African American; leaders, African American; mulatto figures
African Methodist Episcopal church, 92, 95, 97
African-American writers, 2–3, 8. *See also particular authors*
Africanist presence, 5–6, 18, 34
agency, 63, 66, 70
Alice (*Last of the Mohicans*), 11, 16, 23, 28, 29
American Adam figure, 5–6, 18–19
ancestry, 5, 37; in *Last of the Mohicans,* 16–19, 20, 21, 28
Anderson, James D., 94, 95, 131n46
Andrews, William L., 129n1
antebellum era, 7; and Harper, 108, 109–10; mulatto fiction in, 74
antiremoval movement, 7; and abolitionism, 9–10, 12–16
antislavery literature, 31, 38, 39, 47
Aptheker, Herbert, 12
Archy (*The Slave*), 30–31, 35–37, 39–40, 41–47
Archy Moore, the White Slave; or, Memoirs of a Fugitive (Hildreth), 47. *See also The Slave; or, Memoirs of Archy Moore*
Atlantic (periodical), 3

Babb, Valerie, 1–2, 10
Baker, Houston, 3
Bell, Phillip A., 15
Bentley, Nancy, 66
Berkov, Lawrence, 77
Berlant, Lauren, 6
Birney, James G., 14
birth control, 33
blackness: and African American performers, 56; vs. American Adam, 5–6; and the American self, 34; and equality, 60; in *The Grandissimes,* 75, 82, 88; in *Last of the Mohicans,* 18; and sexuality, 86, 88; and slaves, 102; social construction of, 6; and U.S. census, 114; and whiteness, 2, 5, 71, 73, 74, 75, 79–80
Bost, Suzanne, 3
Bras Coupé (*The Grandissimes*), 77–78, 82, 83, 88–89
Brodhead, Richard, 109, 131n55
Brodwin, Stanley, 73
Brothertown Indians (Wisconsin), 15–16, 121n38
Brown, Sterling, 2, 3, 119n4, 120n4
Brown, William Wells, 5, 63, 66, 74
Butler, Octavia, 57, 116–17, 125n25

Cable, George Washington, 5, 8; *The Grandissimes,* 31, 71–90; "Tité Poulette," 75, 83; views of, 75–76, 91, 129n50
Canaday, Nicholas, Jr., 42, 44, 45
Carby, Hazel, 4, 99
Cassy (*The Slave*), 31, 35–37, 39–40, 41
census, U.S., 113–15, 132n4
Chesnutt, Charles, 71; background of, 97, 107–108; and Booker T. Washington, 104, 131n46; on education, 93, 95, 108–109; vs. Harper, 97, 110, 111–12; *Mandy Oxendine,* 3, 8, 91–112
Child, Lydia Maria, 2, 5; background of, 49; *The Christian Indian,* 13; and colonization, 14; and Eden myth, 50–54; and Harper,

63; "The Quadroons," 7, 52–53, 63, 66, 74; and removal policy, 12, 13; *A Romance of the Republic,* 3, 7, 8, 49, 50–61, 63, 65, 69–70, 121n40; on sexual abuse, 31; on *The Slave,* 30; and slavery, 121n40
Chingachook (*Last of the Mohicans*), 16, 23
Chopin, Kate, 71
Christian, Barbara, 99
The Christian Indian; or, The Times of the First Settlers (Child), 13
Christian Recorder (periodical), 3, 69
citizenship: of African Americans, 49–50; and education, 94, 111; in *Iola Leroy,* 100, 105; in *Minnie's Sacrifice,* 61; of Native Americans, 16, 121n38; and racial identity, 4, 8; vs. sovereignty, 16; and whiteness, 16, 113
civil rights, 4, 10, 71, 115; for African American men, 48; and African Americans vs. Native Americans, 21–22; and *Minnie's Sacrifice,* 61, 66, 68, 70
Civil War, 69, 128n14; in *Iola Leroy,* 99, 100, 105; in *Minnie's Sacrifice,* 65, 66, 67–68
civilization, 23, 26, 33, 44, 90. *See also* social order
Clarence (*The Garies and Their Friends*), 31, 42
class: in African American communities, 59–60, 68–69, 81, 92, 96, 97, 99, 104, 108, 109, 130n34, 131n55; and Chesnutt, 109, 111–12; and color, 102, 105–106, 130n34; and culture, 97, 98, 99, 101, 104, 107; and education, 96–97, 103, 107–12, 130n34; and Harper, 110, 111–12; and identity, 2, 109; in *Iola Leroy,* 100, 105, 107–12; in *Mandy Oxendine,* 101, 103–12; in *Minnie's Sacrifice,* 68–69; and namelessness, 34–37; and race, 8, 34, 102, 106, 107; and restraint, 32, 33–34; and self-help, 109–10; and slavery, 20–21; in the South, 34–35; and unified self, 73
Clemen, John, 87
Clotel (Brown), 63, 66, 74
colonization, 21, 116
colonization movement, African American, 14
The Colored American (newspaper), 15
communities, African American, 49, 91–112; and activism, 91; class in, 59–60, 68–69, 81, 92, 96, 97, 99, 104, 108, 109, 130n34, 131n55; culture of, 104, 108, 109, 131n55; duty to, 8, 65, 92, 98, 103–107, 110; and education, 93; in *The Grandissimes,* 89; and Harper, 100, 110; vs. individualism, 100–103; in *Mandy Oxendine,* 102, 103–107; in *Minnie's Sacrifice,* 62–67, 69, 70; mixed-race, 96–97; in *A Romance of the Republic,* 63; teachers in, 94–95, 98–100
Compromise of 1850, 110
Compromise of 1877, 76
Constitution, U.S., amendments to, 48
Cooper, James Fenimore, 7, 45; on Europe vs. America, 20; on Indian-black dichotomy, 21–23, 24; *Last of the Mohicans,* 8, 9–29, 121n40; and miscegenation, 11, 16–19; and removal policy, 12; on slavery-removal link, 20–23, 26
Cora (*Last of the Mohicans*), 7, 10–11; ancestry of, 16–19, 21, 28; as first mulatto, 120n4; and history, 18–19; and Indian-black dichotomy, 23–24; and racial hierarchy, 26–29; and slavery, 19, 28
Creoles, 76–80, 81, 128n14; caste system of, 78–79
Crèvecoeur, Michel de, 29
crossed selves, 72–75; in *The Grandissimes,* 78, 80, 83
culture: of black community, 104, 108, 109, 131n55; and class, 97, 98, 99, 101, 104, 107; Creole, 78–81, 128n14; and mulatto fiction, 116; and Native Americans, 22–23; Old World, 2

Dalke, Ann, 37
Dawn (Butler), 116–17, 125n25
Declaration of Independence, 29
Dekker, George, 11
Delano, Mrs. (*A Romance of the Republic*), 51, 54
democracy, 11, 64, 76, 100; vs. racial ideology, 10, 52; vs. slavery, 12, 49, 127n7
Democracy in America (Tocqueville), 24
Detter, Thomas, 7
domestic vs. public spheres, 64, 110, 111
doubling, 71–90; of consciousness, 64; in *The Grandissimes,* 77, 78–82, 86, 88; in *Pudd'nhead Wilson,* 73–74; of selves, 72–75
Drinnon, Richard, 29
DuBois, W. E. B., 131n46
Ducille, Ann, 3, 7
duty, communal, 8, 110; vs. personal ambition, 92, 98, 103–107

Early, Gerald, 40
economics: and education, 95–96, 98, 103, 104, 126n47, 131n46; of racism, 7, 9; and slavery-removal link, 12, 26
Eden myth: and doubles, 71–90; in *The Grandissimes,* 78–82, 89; in *Iola Leroy,* 100; and masculinity, 45; in *Minnie's Sacrifice,* 64;

and miscegenation, 34, 119n15, 122n47; and mulatto figures, 74–75; and national identity, 5–6, 19, 116; in *Pudd'nhead Wilson,* 73–74; and racial essentialism, 54; in *A Romance of the Republic,* 49, 50–54; and slavery, 19, 20; vs. slavery, 74
education: and activism, 91–92; of African Americans, 56–57, 59, 60, 61, 92–97, 109; Chesnutt on, 93, 95, 108–109; and child labor, 95, 99, 103; and citizenship, 94, 111; and class, 96–97, 103, 107–12, 109, 130n34; and economics, 95–96, 98, 103, 104, 126n47, 131n46; Harper on, 92, 93, 95, 126n47; and industrialization, 95–96, 98, 104, 131n46; in *Iola Leroy,* 92, 93, 105, 107–12; liberal vs. industrial, 95–96, 98, 104, 131n46; in *Mandy Oxendine,* 101, 103; in Reconstruction era, 60, 94, 95, 98; of slaves, 93–94; and teacher training, 95–96; and uplift movement, 93, 94, 95, 96; of women, 99. *See also* teachers
Edward ("The Quadroons"), 52–53
Elder, Arlene, 131n46
Elfenbein, Anna Shannon, 82, 86
Eliza (*Uncle Tom's Cabin*), 31
Elkins, Mary, 105, 130n34
equality: in *The Grandissimes,* 79, 82; in *Minnie's Sacrifice,* 63, 64, 66, 68; vs. paternalism, 59; and race, 56, 60, 90; and wilderness, 45–46; of women, 66
Ernest, John, 130n34
essentialism, racial, 54–57
Europe: imperialism of, 11, 19, 20, 21; in *The Last of the Mohicans,* 7–8, 19–21; and national identity, 2; in *A Romance of the Republic,* 51, 59; as source of slavery, 7–8, 11, 19–21
European Americans, 3; influence of, 23, 24; sexual repression of, 56–57
expansionism, American, 12, 18; and Seminole Wars, 14–15; and slavery-removal link, 22, 26

"A Factor in Human Progress" (Harper), 92, 108
feminism, 6
Fiedler, Leslie, 11, 18
Fishkin, Shelly Fisher, 74
Flora (*A Romance of the Republic*), 50–51, 53–54
Foote, Stephanie, 78
Foster, Frances Smith, 97, 126n42
Franklin, John Hope, 93
free blacks: colonies for, 14; education of, 94, 96; vs. freed, 96; in *The Grandissimes,* 80–81, 87, 89; and Harper, 108, 109–10; and slavery, 81, 110
Freedmen's Bureau, 94, 109
Frisby, James, 86
Frowenfeld (*The Grandissimes*), 76, 78, 80, 81, 84–86, 87
Fugitive Slave Act, 110

Gaines, Kevin, 96
The Garies and Their Friends (Webb), 31, 42
Garrison, William Lloyd, 9–10, 38; and Native American removal, 9, 13–14
gender, 7, 46; in *The Grandissimes,* 75, 87, 89; and Harper vs. Chesnutt, 110–11; in *Minnie's Sacrifice,* 64, 66; in *The Slave,* 31. *See also* men; women
generational differences, 7, 76–77, 111
Genius (periodical), 13–14
George (*Uncle Tom's Cabin*), 31, 42
Gerald (*A Romance of the Republic*), 50–51, 53
Giddings, Joshua, 15
the gothic, 37–41, 88
government, U.S.: and education, 94; laws of, 52, 53, 71, 110, 114; and Native American removal, 12–13; and Seminole Wars, 15; and slavery-removal link, 25–26
The Grandissimes (Cable), 31, 71–90; doubling in, 78–82; Palmyre in, 77–78, 80, 82–89; plot of, 75–78
Green, Beriah, 14
Grimke, Angelina Weld, 14

Haberly, David, 10
Hackenberry, Charles, 97, 129n1
Halttunen, Karen, 38, 39
Harper, Frances E. W., 3, 49–50; background of, 61, 97, 107–108, 109–10; on education, 92, 93, 95, 126n47; "A Factor in Human Progress," 92, 108; *Iola Leroy,* 1, 8, 61, 63, 65, 68, 69, 91–112, 115–16; *Minnie's Sacrifice,* 7, 8, 31, 49, 61–70, 100, 111; *Moses: A Story of the Nile,* 126n42; *Trial and Triumph,* 111
Hector (*The Yemassee*), 23
Heyward (*Last of the Mohicans*), 11, 16, 23
Hildreth, Richard: *Archy Moore, the White Slave,* 47; *The Slave,* 8, 12, 30–47; on the South, 34–35
history: and Cora (*Last of the Mohicans*), 18–19; and Palmyre (*The Grandissimes*), 85
homoeroticism, 40

Honoré and Honoré f.m.c. (*The Grandissimes*), 31, 76–77, 79, 80, 81–82, 83, 84–89
Hopkins, Pauline, 39, 71
Hosmer, H. L., 65, 74
Howard School, 109
Howells, William Dean, 71

identity: bodily, 6; and class, 2, 109; and color, 106; and crossed selves, 72–73; in *The Grandissimes,* 79–80, 82; and incest, 35–37; in *Minnie's Sacrifice,* 64–65; and miscegenation, 57–58; political, 6, 103–104; racial, 49, 54–57, 64, 73, 79; racial vs. national, 1–8; in *A Romance of the Republic,* 49, 54–57; self, 73; and social anxiety, 34–37
illegitimacy, 33, 34
immigrants, 18, 33, 35
imperialism, European, 11, 19, 20, 21
incest, 31, 42; and excess, 39–40; and identity, 35–37
individualism: vs. activism, 100–103; and disjointed selves, 72–73; and race, 111
industrialization, 33, 95–96, 98, 104, 131n46
intertextuality, 7, 62
Iola (*Iola Leroy*), 93, 94, 98–100, 101, 102, 107–108, 110–11
Iola Leroy, or Shadows Uplifted (Harper), 1, 8, 91–112, 115–16; class in, 105, 107–12; education in, 92, 93, 94, 95, 107–12; vs. *Mandy Oxendine,* 101, 102–103, 110–12; vs. *Minnie's Sacrifice,* 61, 63, 65, 68, 69

Jackson, Andrew, 13
Jefferson, Thomas, 12, 24–25
Jim Crow, 4, 78
Joe Christmas (*Uncle Tom's Cabin*), 31
Johnson, Andrew, 50
Jones, Suzanne, 78
Jordan, Winthrop, 22, 34, 119n15, 122n47

Karcher, Carolyn, 2, 50, 55, 57, 58, 59
Kerber, Linda, 14
Ku Klux Klan, 48, 66, 106

The Last of the Mohicans (Cooper), 7–8, 9–29, 121n40; miscegenation in, 10–11, 16–19; racial ideology in, 26–29; slavery-removal link in, 17, 20–23, 26; and *Travelling Bachelor,* 21, 22
laws, 52, 53, 71, 110, 114
leaders, African American: and class, 68–69; community, 91–92; in *The Grandissimes,* 81, 87; and Harper, 108; in *Mandy Oxendine,* 102, 103–104, 105; in *Minnie's Sacrifice,* 63–64, 66; mulatto figures as, 91–92, 97; teachers as, 8, 91–112; women vs. men as, 110–11
legitimacy, 6, 8, 86, 114
Letters from an American Farmer (Crèvecoeur), 29
Lewis, Vashti, 99
The Liberator (periodical), 13, 30, 38; masthead of, 9–10
Louis (*Minnie's Sacrifice*), 31, 61–62, 67–68, 69, 70
Louisiana, 76–77, 78
Louisiana Purchase, 12
Lowell, James Russell, 14
Lowry (*Mandy Oxendine*), 93, 101–107
Lundy, Benjamin, 14
Lusane, Clarence, 113
lynching, 71, 89, 106–107, 114

Madison, James, 12
Magua (*Last of the Mohicans*), 16, 26–27, 28, 29
Malchow, H. L., 39
Mandy (*Mandy Oxendine*), 101, 103, 106, 107
Mandy Oxendine (Chesnutt), 3, 8, 91–112; and Chesnutt's experience, 97; class in, 103–12; dates of, 91, 129n1; education in, 92, 93, 107–12; individualism in, 100–103; vs. *Iola Leroy,* 105, 110–12
Marcus, George E., 72–73
Marcus, Steven, 38
marriage, 56, 58, 103; interracial, 59, 69, 115–16; vs. social confusion, 36–37. *See also* miscegenation
Martin (*The Slave*), 44
masculinity: in *The Slave,* 41–47; and violence, 25–26, 41–47
masturbation, 33
Mayer, Magdalene, 27
McDowell, Deborah, 3, 99
medical literature, 33
men: African-American, 48, 58, 72, 75, 87, 88, 89; and black women, 86, 87; as leaders, 110–11; mulatto, 127n50; and violence, 25–26, 41–47; white, 86, 87; and white women, 89
middle class: African-American, 69, 92, 98, 105, 111; and sexual restraint, 33; as teachers, 99, 101; and uplift, 92, 102; white, 60, 83–84; vs. working class, 98, 105, 111
Mills, Bruce, 51
Minnie (*Minnie's Sacrifice*), 61–62, 63, 64, 65–67, 69, 111

Minnie's Sacrifice (Harper), 7, 8, 31, 61–70, 100, 111; African American community in, 62–67, 69, 70; vs. *Iola Leroy,* 61, 63, 65, 68, 69; national reconciliation in, 49, 62–63, 64, 65, 67–70; and *A Romance of the Republic,* 69–70
miscegenation: Cable on, 129n50; and Eden myth, 34, 119n15, 122n47; as gene trade, 57–58, 59; in *Last of the Mohicans,* 10–11, 16–19; laws against, 53; and polygenesis theory, 113–14; and racelessness, 57–58; and readability of body, 6; in *A Romance of the Republic,* 49, 57–61; and social anxiety, 35
Missouri territory, 12
Monroe, James, 13
Moore, Colonel (*The Slave*), 31, 35, 36, 37, 40, 41
Morgan, Thomas J., 95
Morrison, Toni, 2, 6, 18, 34; *Playing in the Dark,* 5, 123n21, 127n7
Moses: A Story of the Nile (poem; Harper), 126n42
Moses, story of, 50, 63, 64, 70, 126n42
Moss, Alfred A., Jr., 93
"The Mulatto" (Sejour), 39
mulatto fiction: and abolitionism, 32–33; and doubled/crossed selves, 74–75; and *Minnie's Sacrifice,* 62–63, 69; and national identity, 116; in post-Reconstruction era, 71, 91; and *Pudd'nhead Wilson,* 74; racial discovery in, 65; in Reconstruction era, 48–49, 70, 74; and sexuality, 32–34; and *The Slave,* 31, 47
mulatto figures: and bondage, 86–87; choices of, 115–16; Cora as first, 120n4; as doubled selves, 72; in Eden, 74–75; in Harper vs. Chesnutt, 111; and individualism, 100–103; as leaders, 91–92, 97; male, 127n50; and national identity, 1–8, 47, 69, 113, 115–16; and passing, 46, 101–102, 103; and pornography, 38–39; and racism, 2, 4, 89–90; and social anxiety, 35, 47; stereotypes of, 2, 3, 42–43; as teachers, 92, 98–100; tragic, 2–3, 53, 66, 119n4, 126n50; and white audiences, 2–3, 99
Munro (*Last of the Mohicans*), 16, 17–18, 19–20, 23

national identity, American: and American Adam figure, 5–6, 18–19; and blackness, 34; and doubled/crossed selves, 72, 74; and Eden myth, 5–6, 19, 116; vs. European, 20; in *Last of the Mohicans,* 11, 18, 19; and masculinity, 45; in *Minnie's Sacrifice,* 61, 65; and mulatto figures, 1–8, 47, 69, 113, 115–16; multiracial, 64, 65; and national reconciliation, 54; and Native Americans, 11, 20, 22–23, 29, 121n37; and race, 1–8, 9–10, 13, 14, 52, 90, 100, 113–17; and *A Romance of the Republic,* 51; and slavery, 4, 34; and slavery-removal link, 25–26; and whiteness, 2, 10, 11, 72
national reconciliation, 54; in *Minnie's Sacrifice,* 49, 62–63, 64, 65, 67–70
Native American removal: and Indian-black dichotomy, 24–26; in *Last of the Mohicans,* 17, 20–23, 26; movement against, 7, 9–10, 12–16; and Seminole Wars, 14–15; slavery linked to, 12–16, 17, 20–23, 25–26, 27, 29
Native Americans: and abolitionism, 7–8, 13–14; and African Americans, 14, 15–16, 21–29; as aliens, 10; citizenship of, 16, 121n38; conflict with, 20, 29; in *Last of the Mohicans,* 7–8, 9–29; and national identity, 11, 20, 22–23, 29, 121n37; in racial hierarchy, 26–27; treaties with, 9, 10; in U.S. census, 114; violence of, 21–22, 23, 27, 29
Natty (*Last of the Mohicans*), 16, 20, 23, 29, 45; as American Adam, 18–19
Neighbor Jackwood (Trowbridge), 65
Nelson, Dana, 56
Newlyn, Andrea K., 51
Nobles, Melissa, 113, 132n4
Notes on the State of Virginia (Jefferson), 25

"Octoroon Slave of Cuba" (Detter), 7
Of One Blood (Hopkins), 39
Osherow, Michele, 116

Palmyre (*The Grandissimes*), 77–78, 80, 82–89, 128n18
passing, 46, 101–102, 103
paternalism, 68, 81, 97, 105; in *A Romance of the Republic,* 58–61, 69
patriarchy, African American, 72, 87, 88
Payne, Daniel Alexander, 94
Pease, Donald, 19
Pennsylvania Freeman (newspaper), 13
Peterson, Carla, 98
Philadelphia National Enquirer (newspaper), 13
Playing in the Dark: Whiteness and the Literary Imagination (Morrison), 5, 123n21, 127n7
politics, 6, 64, 94; and slavery, 12–16; teachers in, 95, 103–104
polygenesis theory, 113–14, 132n4
pornography: and the gothic, 37–41; of pain, 38

Porter, Kenneth Wiggins, 14, 15
post-Reconstruction era, 8, 71, 91, 95; and *The Grandissimes,* 76, 78; and *Iola Leroy,* 110; and *Minnie's Sacrifice,* 65
power: and abolitionism, 32, 38; and masculinity, 42, 43, 46; in *A Romance of the Republic,* 60; and slavery, 18, 32
prostitution, 33, 34, 126n47
public vs. domestic space, 64, 110, 111
Pudd'nhead Wilson (Twain), 73–74, 76, 89

"The Quadroons" (Child), 7, 52–53, 63, 66, 74

race: categorization by, 49, 57, 69, 73, 74, 91, 100, 113–15; and class, 8, 34, 102, 106, 107; in Creole culture, 78–80; and crossed selves, 72–73; and equality, 56, 60, 90; and gender, 75; ideology of, 1, 3, 4, 6–7, 9–10, 23, 26–29, 114–15; vs. individualism, 111; in *Last of the Mohicans,* 23, 26–29; in *Mandy Oxendine,* 101; and national identity, 1–8, 9–10, 13, 14, 52, 90, 100, 113–17; in post-Reconstruction era, 71; purity of, 5; readability of, 6, 114; in Reconstruction era, 48; social construction of, 1, 113, 116; and social order, 37; in U.S. census, 113–15; and violence, 106–107
racelessness, 5–6, 57–58
racism: vs. democracy, 49; economics of, 7, 9; and education, 93, 96, 107; in Europe, 59; in *The Grandissimes,* 75, 76, 80, 81, 87, 88; vs. individualism, 101; in *Minnie's Sacrifice,* 66, 68; and mulatto characters, 2, 4, 89–90; vs. national identity, 13, 14, 90; and paternalism, 58; resistance to, 8; in *A Romance of the Republic,* 50, 54; and slavery, 20, 89–90; Twain on, 73, 74; and U.S. census, 115; in women's movement, 48
Reconstruction, 7, 8, 48–70; and Chesnutt, 109; education in, 60, 94, 95, 98; failure of, 81, 89, 93; in *The Grandissimes,* 78, 81; in *Iola Leroy,* 110; in *Minnie's Sacrifice,* 62–67, 70; mulatto fiction in, 48–49, 70, 74; mulatto-black relations in, 97; and national reconciliation, 54; racism in, 50; in *A Romance of the Republic,* 70; Twain on, 74
Redemption. *See* post-Reconstruction era
religion: and African Methodist Episcopal church, 92, 95, 97; and masculinity, 43–44; in *Minnie's Sacrifice,* 69; vs. social confusion, 36–37
repression, 56–57, 88
Reynolds, David, 37–38
A Romance of the Republic (Child), 3, 7, 8, 50–61, 63; and Cable, 74; Eden myth in, 50–54; and Harper, 65; and *Last of the Mohicans,* 121n40; and *Minnie's Sacrifice,* 69–70; miscegenation in, 49, 57–61
Rosa (*A Romance of the Republic*), 50–51, 53–54
Rosalie ("The Quadroons"), 52–53
Rose Amelia (*Mandy Oxendine*), 105–106
Rosenberg, Charles, 33, 42
Rubin, Louis, 85

Sabbath schools, 95, 99
Sánchez-Eppler, Karen, 6
Sargent, John O., 30
science fiction, 116–17
Scribner's Monthly (periodical), 75
Sedgwick, Catherine Maria, 12
segregation, 4, 71, 93; in *The Grandissimes,* 76; in *Mandy Oxendine,* 103; and polygenesis theory, 113, 114
Sejour, Victor, 39
self-help, 92, 96, 108; and class, 109–10; and women, 110–11. *See also* uplift movement
Seminole Negroes, 14–15
Seminole Wars, 14–15
sexuality: and abolitionism, 32–33; and blackness, 86, 88; and bondage, 86–87, 88; excess in, 36, 39–40; gothic, 37–41; in *Last of the Mohicans,* 11; and mulatto fiction, 32–34; of Palmyre (*The Grandissimes*), 84–89; and racial essentialism, 55–57; in *A Romance of the Republic,* 57; in *The Slave,* 31; and slavery, 18, 65, 67, 85, 89; and social anxiety, 33, 35–37, 40–41; and tragic mulatta, 126n50; and transcendence, 66–67, 127n50; and violence, 5, 32, 38, 39, 40, 66–67
siblings, 8, 71, 72; in *The Grandissimes,* 74–75, 77, 82; in *Minnie's Sacrifice,* 64; in *The Slave,* 31. *See also* incest
Simm, William Gilmore, 23
The Slave; or, Memoirs of Archy Moore (Hildreth), 8, 12, 30–47; the gothic in, 37–41; masculinity in, 41–47; social anxiety in, 34–37
slavery: and class, 20–21; vs. democracy, 12, 49, 127n7; and doubled/crossed selves, 72, 75; vs. Eden myth, 19, 20, 74; end of, 48; Europe as source of, 7–8, 11, 19–21; and free blacks, 81, 110; in *The Grandissimes,* 75, 78; and Indian-black dichotomy, 23,

24–26; in *Iola Leroy,* 93, 100, 110; in *Last of the Mohicans,* 7, 8, 9, 11, 16, 17, 18, 26; in *Mandy Oxendine,* 102; in *Minnie's Sacrifice,* 61; and mulatto characters, 4, 5; and national identity, 4, 34, 35; and Native American removal, 12–16, 17, 20–23, 25–26, 27, 29; politics of, 12–16; and pornography, 38, 40; and power, 18, 32; and *Pudd'nhead Wilson,* 73–74; and racism, 20, 89–90; in *A Romance of the Republic,* 49, 50, 54, 69, 121n40; and Seminole Wars, 14–15; and sexuality, 18, 37, 58, 65, 67, 85, 89
slaves: and blackness, 102; education of, 93–94, 99; escaped, 15, 25; vs. free blacks, 81, 96; and Harper, 108; and masculinity, 42, 43–44, 46; population of, 12
Slotkin, Richard, 22, 46
Smith, W. W., 5, 74
social anxiety: and the gothic, 39; and mulattos, 35, 47; and namelessness, 34–37; and sexuality, 33, 35–37, 40–41
social order, 5, 71, 96; vs. anarchy, 40–41; and restraint, 32; and sexuality, 33
social restraint: and abolitionism, 32–33; and anxiety, 37; and class, 33–34; and masculinity, 42, 43–44
Sollors, Werner, 3, 5, 36, 42
the South: and abolitionism, 32, 33; class in, 34–35; education in, 95, 131n46; in *The Grandissimes,* 76–77; loyalty to, 67–68; lynching in, 106–107; and Native American removal, 12; post-Reconstruction, 71, 73; Reconstruction-era, 48; violence in, 66, 67
Stanton, Elizabeth Cady, 48
stereotypes, 4, 96, 99; of mulattos, 2, 3, 42–43
Still, William, 97, 126n47
Stokes, Mason, 34
Stowe, Harriet Beecher, 14, 42, 43; *Uncle Tom's Cabin,* 31, 47, 67
suffrage: for African-American men, 48; for women, 48, 66
the supernatural, 71, 77, 78, 88

Tamenund, Chief (*Last of the Mohicans*), 26–27, 28
Tappan, Arthur, 14
teachers: as activists, 93, 94–95, 98; and class, 97; and Harper, 108, 110; as leaders, 8, 91–112; mulatto figures as, 92, 98–100; in politics, 95, 103–104; as race representatives, 95, 98, 104, 110; and self-help, 109–10
temperance, 33, 61, 108
Thomas (*The Slave*), 43–44, 45
Thoughts on African Colonization (Garrison), 14
"Tité Poulette" (Cable), 75, 83
Tocqueville, Alexis de, 13, 24
Tompkins, Jane, 4, 10
the tragic mulatto, 2–3, 53, 119n4; female, 66, 126n50
transcendence: and motherhood, 67; and sexuality, 66–67, 127n50
The Travelling Bachelor; or, Notions of the Americans (Cooper), 20–22, 24
Trial and Triumph (Harper), 111
Trowbridge, John, 65
The Truth Teller (periodical), 47
Tucker, George, 14
Twain, Mark, 5, 71; *Pudd'nhead Wilson,* 73–74, 76, 89

Uncas (*Last of the Mohicans*), 11, 16, 23
Uncle Tom's Cabin (Stowe), 31, 47, 67
uplift movement, 91–92, 99, 108; and education, 93, 94, 95, 96. *See also* self-help

violence: and education, 93; in *The Grandissimes,* 78, 81–82, 87, 88; lynching, 71, 89, 106–107, 114; and masculinity, 25–26, 41–47; of Native Americans, 21–22, 23, 27, 29; in post-Reconstruction era, 71; in Reconstruction era, 48; regeneration through, 45–46; sexualized, 5, 32, 38, 39, 40, 66–67; in *The Slave,* 31, 40, 41–47; and white males, 127n50; and wilderness, 45–46

Walker, Cheryl, 16, 121n37
Walker, Peter, 32
Walter, Ronald, 32
Washington, Booker T., 104, 131n46
Webb, Frank, 42, 43
Weld, Theodore, 14
white audiences, 2–3, 55–56, 59, 62, 69, 99
whiteness, 60, 86, 102, 115; and blackness, 2, 5, 71, 73, 74, 75, 79–80; and citizenship, 16, 113; and crossed selves, 72–73; in *The Grandissimes,* 75, 79, 82; in *Last of the Mohicans,* 16, 18, 19; and miscegenation, 57–58; and national identity, 2, 10, 11, 72; and racelessness, 5–6
Whittier, John Greenleaf, 13
wilderness, 45–46

William Watkins Academy, 97
Williamson, Joel, 97
Wilson, Kimberly A. C., 69
women: agency of, 66; black, 86, 87, 99; and class, 69; education of, 99; and miscegenation, 58; in public space, 64, 110, 111; white, 28–29, 83, 88, 89; white vs. black, 56, 83–84
women's movement, 48, 49, 61
Woodson, Carter G., 15
Wright, J. Leitch, 24

Xarifa ("The Quadroons"), 52–53

The Yankee Slave Driver (Smith), 74
Yellin, Jean Fagan, 3
The Yemassee (Simms), 23
Young, Robert, 23, 25

Cassandra Jackson is Assistant Professor of English at Northeastern University in Boston.